4G: Deployment Strategies and Operational Implications

Trichy Venkataraman Krishnamurthy

Rajaneesh Shetty

Apress®

4G: Deployment Strategies and Operational Implications

ISBN-13 (pbk): 978-1-4302-6325-8

ISBN-13 (electronic): 978-1-4302-6326-5

Managing Director: Welmoed Spahr
Lead Editor: Nikhil Chinnari
Technical Reviewers: Biljana Badic and Annam Kishore
Editorial Board: Steve Anglin, Gary Cornell, Louise Corrigan, Jonathan Gennick, Robert Hutchinson, Michelle Lowman, James Markham, Matthew Moodie, Jeff Olson, Jeffrey Pepper, Douglas Pundick, Ben Renow-Clarke, Gwenan Spearing, Matt Wade, Steve Weiss
Coordinating Editor: Mark Powers
Copy Editor: Mary Bearden
Compositor: SPi Global
Indexer: SPi Global
Artist: SPi Global
Cover Designer: Anna Ishchenko

Distributed to the book trade worldwide by Springer Science+Business Media New York, 233 Spring Street, 6th Floor, New York, NY 10013. Phone 1-800-SPRINGER, fax (201) 348-4505, e-mail orders-ny@springer-sbm.com, or visit www.springeronline.com. Apress Media, LLC is a California LLC and the sole member (owner) is Springer Science + Business Media Finance Inc (SSBM Finance Inc). SSBM Finance Inc is a Delaware corporation.

For information on translations, please e-mail rights@apress.com, or visit www.apress.com.

Apress and friends of ED books may be purchased in bulk for academic, corporate, or promotional use. eBook versions and licenses are also available for most titles. For more information, reference our Special Bulk Sales–eBook Licensing web page at www.apress.com/bulk-sales.

Any source code or other supplementary material referenced by the author in this text is available to readers at www.apress.com/9781430263258. For detailed information about how to locate your book's source code, go to www.apress.com/source-code.

To my parents
To Ramya for all love and support
To Advu & Advi for bearing with appa
To SG Ganesh for inspiring me

—Trichy Venkataraman Krishnamurthy

This book is dedicated to my dear father Sudhakar Shetty, my mother Veena,
my dear wife, Rashmi, and my two little sons Aarav and Atharv who
have been and remain to be my inspiration and support.

—Rajaneesh Shetty

Contents at a Glance

Contents

About the Authors

T. V. Krishnamurthy has worked in the telecommunications industry for more than 15 years. He has been strongly involved in radio technologies for nearly a decade while working with Siemens communications and Nokia Siemens networks and now the Radisys Corporation. He has been involved in varying roles from software development to team leadership to feature specifications and architecture work and project management, with varied radio technologies like 3G-RNC, WCDMA BTS, WiMAX BTS, and now recently LTE. He has also worked in specifying and developing features for Internet HSPA. His interests include software engineering, requirements engineering, QoS, and scheduler implementations. He also has published papers in the areas of knowledge management and software engineering. He holds an IEEE CSDP certification and is a qualified CSDP trainer, a practicing PMI certified project management professional (PMP), and a PMP trainer. He lives and works out of Bangalore, India.

Rajaneesh Shetty is a telecom specialist with nearly 13 years of continuous and progressive international (multicultural) experience in development and testing lifecycle of telecom products using state-of-the-art technologies, with positions spanning development to technical leadership and management. He has worked on telecom projects with Infosys in core networks, Nokia Siemens networks in radio networks, and now in RMA (radio mobile access) with LTE solutions. He has experience in diverse network technologies such as LTE-TDD, LTE-FDD, UMTS, 3G, GSM, GPRS, HSPA, RRC, MAC, layer 3, core networks, HLR, IN, and billing. He has rich experience in various activities like feature analysis, specification, development, integration, and testing. He has also been involved in technical management of telecom system projects. His current interests include LTE system testing strategies, self-organizing networks, and enhanced customer experience. He lives and works out of Bangalore, India.

Introduction

This book evaluates a range of design and deployment strategies for LTE network business development, and presents a process for planning and evolving network roadmaps.

Among those who will find this book useful are new field engineers who have been entrusted with the arduous tasks of deploying 4G networks. The initial chapter in the book endeavors to arm you with enough information to understand what you are doing, and why. The book also demonstrates how self-organizing networks (SON) can help improve the deployment process and help reduce the round trip time in optimizing and tuning your network. Subsequent chapters cover roadmap development and how it improves your ability to plan, build, and deploy more successful networks.

From a broader perspective, this book is for all people involved or entrusted with the maintenance of 4G networks, including architects, product managers, and program managers. Senior management executives will also find the book valuable, as it give them the requisite knowledge to better ensure that relevant stakeholders are involved in the process of roadmap management and evolve strategies to ensure that their 4G networks remain operational, meaningful, and successful. We cover potential roadblocks to successful deployments, and how to avoid or overcome them. We also delve into roadmap management, with suggestions on how to keep them relevant using reliability engineering, organizational culture, and evolution concepts.

How This Book Is Structured

Chapter 1, "Network Planning," covers the nuts and bolts of deployment, and gives a speedy tour of the whole process.

Chapter 2, "Self-Organizing Networks and LTE Deployment," gives a general overview of SON concepts, and helps explain how SON attempts to solve various deployment issues.

Chapter 3, "Deployment Challenges in Evolving 4G," introduces readers to the challenges of LTE deployment, and highlights trends in user and traffic profiles , as well as newer trends like the Internet of Things, which need to be accounted for by LTE networks.

Chapter 4, "Network Roadmaps," introduces roadmap concepts for networks and provides further coverage of factors that can affect stakeholders.

Chapter 5, "Network Roadmap Evolution," focuses on how network roadmaps have to evolve and adapt to changes in technology, markets, deployments, and traffic patterns.

Chapter 6, "A Process for Network Roadmaps Evolution," presents a detailed set of processes for network roadmap management and evolution.

Prerequisites

For the deployment-related sections of the book, readers are expected to have knowledge of LTE and radio basics, and have some practical idea of what is to be accomplished. For sections covering network roadmap management and evolution, readers should have a basic understanding of network product development.

CHAPTER 1

▧ ▧ ▧

Network Planning

Network planning, especially for a cellular network, can be an extremely complex as well as time-consuming procedure. There are many steps and parameters that should be considered to ensure a well-planned radio network.

This chapter gives a fast tour through the network planning and optimization of a Long Term Evolution (LTE) radio network. We also present a strong grounding through the various aspects of the LTE standard and features that you can use as a guide through the various options for deployment. This will equip you with the knowledge to understand the choices you can make when selecting a system and need to shortlist solutions. In some cases, you may already understand the options based on decisions you have already made for network options using some other method.

We start by going through some basic concepts and steps that should be followed for deployment of any radio technology. After covering these basics, we deal with the different aspects of LTE features in terms of the deployment impact in the dimensions of coverage, capacity, and performance.

We then cover some advanced features intended to make LTE deployments easier. We also cover the various services offered and what types of implications these hold for the solution being deployed. We revisit the generic topics of deployment with LTE radio frequency (RF)–specific deployment inputs and discuss issues that can arise during that process.

Finally, we end the chapter with inputs on the performance matrix and how the different aspects of LTE-evolved node B (eNodeB) performance can be tested.

The main goal in network planning is to ensure that the planned area is covered completely. Every cellular network needs cell-site planning to ensure coverage requirements, to maximize capacity requirements, and to avoid interference. The cell-planning process consists of many different tasks, which together make it possible to achieve a well-working network. The major activities involved in the cell-planning process are represented in Figure 1-1. Broadly, the radio network planning and optimization activity can be subclassified into the following phases:

- Dimensioning phase

- Planning and implementation phase

- Optimization phase

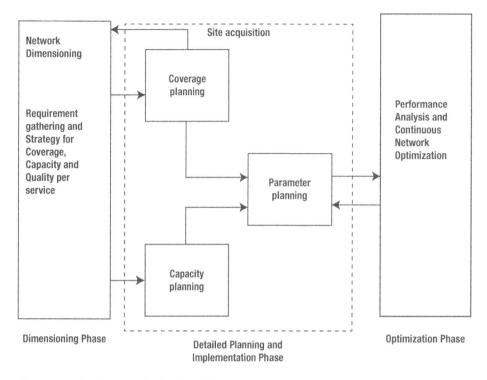

Figure 1-1. *Radio network planning phases*

Dimensioning Phase

The dimensioning phase will mainly involve information and requirement gathering from the customer from which the initial objectives for the radio network planning can be set. Some of the key inputs that are considered or required to be performed in the dimensioning are outlined in the sections that follow.

Configuration for the Site

As part of the configuration details, it is important to understand whether the site will be configured for a multiple-input and multiple-output (MIMO) or single-input and single-output (SISO) system. If the system is MIMO, then the transmission mode needs configuration. Also, as a part of site configuration, it is important to understand how many cells will be installed or eNodeB (i.e., sector configuration) for each site.

User and Traffic Volume Estimation

As a part of dimensioning, it is important to estimate the user volume and the traffic volume for each site; for example, the number of users in an urban site will be very high compared with the volume for a rural site. Similarly, the traffic volume will be higher in an area that has small offices set up in comparison with a highway deployment. The user and traffic volume estimation directly impacts the cell size that can be supported for a particular area and the capacity requirement. It also is useful for parameter settings like physical random access channel (PRACH) configuration settings, scheduler settings, and so forth. Apart from the traffic volume, it is also important to understand the traffic type that will dominate the cell so the dimensioning can be done accordingly by calculating the net bit rate for the traffic type, 4G voice over Internet protocol traffic (VOIP), streaming traffic, hypertext transfer protocol (HTTP) traffic, and so forth.

Coverage and Capacity Estimation

The customer should be able to provide the information on the area that is planned for service and also the quality of service offered for each user terminal (UE) within the service area. With this input from the customer, the cell coverage and capacity estimates are performed. Radio link budgeting is performed to understand the cell size that can be achieved with the input given from which the number of sites or cells required to plan the network area can be determined.

Interface Requirement

The interface requirements mainly deal with the S1 (interface between the mobility management entity [MME] and eNodeB) and X2 interface (interface between two eNodeBs) dimensioning. Based on the number of sites required (derived from the link budget activity) and the operator's allocated budget, the interfaces for each eNodeB will be dimensioned.

Budget Information

Budget information is very important because the number of resources (hardware) can be derived from the this, and in cases of limited budgets, the capacity or coverage planning will need to be accomplished with limited resources for a given area. Figure 1-2 presents a flow chart of the budget planning process.

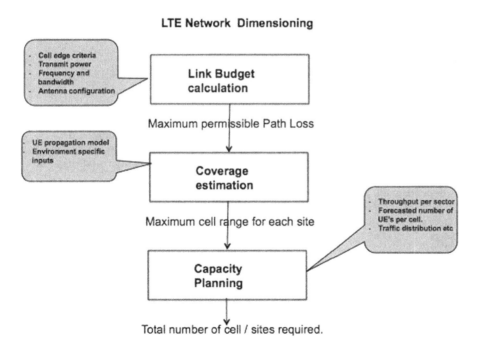

Figure 1-2. *Network dimensioning based on budget*

Planning and Implementation Phase

In the dimensioning phase, the equipment requirements are determined based on the number of cells or sites needed to provide a network to the complete area. During the planning and implementation phase, the exact location of where these eNodeBs should be placed is determined. Site selection activity is performed to accomplish the planning done in the dimensioning phase.

Upon determination of the sites where the eNodeBs will need to be placed, the network planning tools (i.e., Mentum, atoll) can be used to reconfirm that the capacity and the coverage planning that was performed in the dimensioning phase has been accomplished.

During the planning phase, backhaul planning must also be done. In cases where the site is a colocated site, the backhaul planning should be carried out for both colocates as well as the new site.

Parameter planning and setting is a major part of this phase. Some of the parameters that will impact the coverage and capacity planning are:

- Uplink/downlink (UL/DL) frequency

- Bandwidth of operation

- Transmission mode

- Transmission power

- Quality of service (QoS) parameters

- Population distribution and density

- Outdoor environment type (urban, rural, small office, residential, etc.)

- Maps and clutter details for the area

- Fading model type (Extended Vehicular A model [EVA], Extended Typical Urban model [ETU], Extended Pedestrian A model [EPA], etc.)

- Predicted traffic type and its distribution

These factors will be discussed in detail later as they all impact the capacity and coverage planning.

As part of the planning process, signal-to-interference-plus-noise ratio (SINR) vs. throughput mapping is performed for different propagation models (i.e., EVA, ETU, EPA, etc.) and for different transmission modes (spatial multiplexing, transmit diversity, etc.).

Cell edge definition would depend on the SINR mapping.

Optimization Phase

Once the planning and implementation are complete, it is very common practice to run drive tests for the planned sites. Drive tests verify the predictions made by the planning tools, and the results from the drive tests are compared against the results from the simulations. Fine tuning is performed after the drive tests to ensure that the deviation in the results between simulation and drive tests is minimal.

A part of the drive test, parameters like reference signal receive power (RSRP), reference signal received quality (RSRQ), or SINR the UL and DL throughputs at different points of the cell are noted. The results are then compared with the SNR predictions made by the planning tool and deviations are noted and tuned wherever required.

Coverage Planning

Coverage planning targets for the complete service area are tested to ensure there are no coverage holes (i.e., the UE never experiences a no-service condition within the entire service area). Coverage plans, however, do not take into consideration any quality of service that the user experiences within a cell or site. The end aim is to provide the count of the resources or eNodeBs and cells that are required for the complete service area.

Some of the most important aspects that need to be considered as a part of the coverage planning are:

1. *The eNodeB transmitting power and the type of cell that is being planned.* The eNodeB transmitting power is the key for any coverage planning, and the transmitting power will vary based on the cell size. For example, a macro cell will have a transmission power of 10 watts per port (40 watts per cell in cases of MIMO cells). The DL coverage cell radius should be derived based on the transmission power of the antenna added with the gains (antenna gain, diversity gain, etc.) with the assumption of path loss (receiver loss, propagation loss, etc.). Cell radius calculation will be covered in detail in the link budget calculation section.

2. *The eNodeB receiver sensitivity.* In the uplink, in order to calculate the cell radius, one of the most important parameters that the operator relies on is the receiver sensitivity of the eNodeB. The eNodeB receiver sensitivity is a deciding factor for the maximum allowed path loss between the UE and the eNodeB in the uplink direction, beyond which the eNodeB cannot differentiate accurately between signal and noise. Better receiver sensitivity of the eNodeB will directly result in a larger cell radius (coverage radius) in the uplink. The 3GPP 36.141 defines the test for deriving the reference sensitivity of a receiver. The specification also requires that a receiver sensitivity of less than -100.8 decibel milliwatts (dbm) is acceptable. However, many vendors have a receiver sensitivity value of around -102 dbm or better.

3. *UE receiver sensitivity and transmission power.* Similar to the eNodeB receiver sensitivity, UE receiver sensitivity is an important factor in determining the DL cell radius for coverage planning. Typically for a macro cell, the UL cell radius will be a limiting factor in comparison with the DL cell radius simply because of the difference in the transmission powers. In LTE category 2 UE and onward, the maximum uplink transmit power is 23 db.

4. *Terrain.* Terrain is an important consideration for any site planning and will impact the absorption or attenuation capability of a site. For example, a site with irregular heights will not have linear loss and is subjected to shadow areas or reflection, whereas a site with fairly regular height will have a more predictable linear loss. Similarly, the indoor to outdoor ratio of a site also makes a difference when it comes to cell radius calculation (i.e., the penetration losses for an indoor user is higher compared with that for an outdoor user); therefore, planning an urban cell will be subject to more losses due to a higher percentage of indoor to outdoor users in comparison with a rural cell.

Improving Coverage for a Given Service Area

Some common practices to improve the coverage for a given service area are:

- *Receiver selection.* Selecting an eNodeB with a better receiver sensitivity will help to improve the coverage for a service area.

- *Implementing receiver diversity.* In UL highers, the chances of correctly decoding the received signal from the UE improve the coverage.

- *Beamforming.* For uneven heights, beamforming can be a very handy feature to compensate for any coverage hole.

- *Improving the antenna gain.* This is particularly useful for smaller cells, wherein the DL cell radius is limited in comparison with the UL cell radius.

- *Adding more sites.* In case none of these techniques can be used to compensate for a coverage hole, the last option would be to add a new site.

Capacity Planning

The capacity of an eNodeB indicates the maximum number of users that can be served by the eNodeB with a desired quality of service or the maximum cell throughput that can be achieved for a particular site at a given time. Increasing the capacity would mean increasing the number of users that can be accommodated by a cell or eNodeB, which in turn means that the number of eNodeBs or cells required to accommodate a volume of users inside a given area would be lessened, thereby reducing the cost of deployment for an operator.

Capacity planning, like coverage planning, also aims at providing an estimate on the number of resources or eNodeBs required for a given service area. However, in capacity planning, the quality of service that is provided to the users within the service area is the key factor.

Typically, the resource calculation from capacity planning for a given service area is higher in comparison with the resource calculations made by coverage planning. Capacity planning is initially done by using a simulation tool (e.g., Opnet, Radiodim tool, etc.), which takes in various parameters and plots an SINR graph for a UE at different distances from the transmitter. The simulations are performed to at least derive these results:

- Average throughput for a close-range user

- Average throughput for a midrange user

- Average throughput for a far-range user

- Number of UEs that can be placed inside the cell with a throughput for each UE above the acceptable levels.

With these results and an estimate on the total number of users within the service area, the total number of cells that would be required can be calculated.

Later, during the drive test phase, some of these tests are repeated and the SINR plotting is performed at the actual site and matched with the simulated results for accuracy.

Improve Capacity for a Particular Service Area

Some of the common practices to improve the capacity for a given service area are:

Adding more cells. Adding more cells to the service area would mean that the number of UEs that need to be accommodated by a single cell will be reduced, therefore, the quality of service for each UE can be achieved.

More sectors for a site. This again would mean adding more cells to the planned area; however, this activity involves sectorization for specific sites that provide service to a larger number of users with higher traffic.

MIMO implementation. MIMO features enable capacity within a service area, and spatial multiplexing ensures that the user's throughput (in good channel conditions) is improved. The transmit diversity feature ensures the same for UEs in poor channel conditions. Also, there are advanced MIMO features like beamforming that target improvement of UE throughput, thereby enhancing the capacity of a particular cell.

Increasing bandwidth. Another method to increase the capacity of a cell is to increase the bandwidth of the frequency. This method is very expensive and not very practical.

Radio Link Budget for LTE

Radio link budgeting is where the maximum permissible path loss is calculated for a planned site. Budgeting is done in both UL as well as DL directions, and the cell radius is calculated for either capacity or coverage in both the directions and the minimal cell radius is decided upon.

The link budget calculation depends on various parameters on the transmitter end or the receiver end, which contribute to the effective path loss calculation as presented in the equation:

$$PL = Tx\ Power + Tx\ Gain + Rx\ Gain - Tx\ Loss - Rx\ Loss,$$

where PL is the total path loss of the signal in decibels, Tx Power is the transmission power in decibel milliWatts, Tx Gain is the transmitter gain (antenna gain) in decibels, Rx Gain is the receiver gain (antenna gain) in decibels, Tx Loss is the transmitter loss in decibels, and Rx Loss is the receiver losses in decibels. Figure 1-3 diagrams this process.

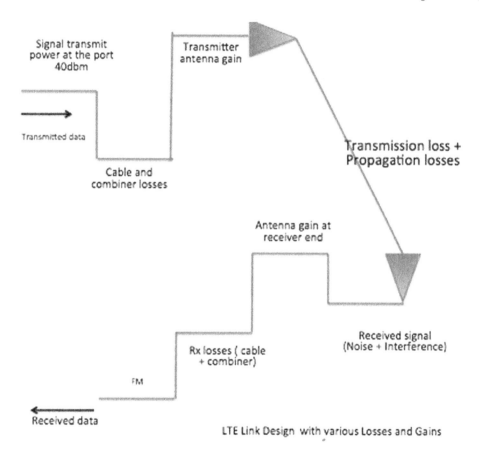

Figure 1-3. *Process of gains and losses in transmission path*

Transmission Power

Transmission power is the key to any link budget calculation. The higher the transmission power, the higher the permissible path loss and the greater the cell radius.

Depending on the cell size, the transmission powers are of different levels, for example, a macro cell transmits at 10 to 20 watts per port, whereas for a pico cell, the power would be in the range of 2 watts.

Radio link budgeting is performed separately for the UL and DL as the transmission power of the signal will be of different power levels (i.e., the maximum UE transmit power is around 23 db, which is used for radio link budget calculation or acceptable path loss calculation for the UL).

Features like MIMO increase the transmission power of the antenna and therefore increase the coverage and capacity of the cell.

Antenna Gains

Antenna gains, especially on the transmitter side (eNodeB antenna gain), are the most significant gain contributors for a link budget calculation. The reason for the gain is because of the directional behavior of the antenna (i.e., the power emitted or received by the antennas is focused in one particular direction). For a macro site, typically the antenna gain is in the order of around 18 dbm and the receiver gain on the UE side is in the order of 0 or 1 dbm. If there is no external antenna for the UE, then the gain is 0.

Diversity Gain

Diversity on the receiver side is useful when decoding the original signal, especially at the cell edge where the path loss is higher. The diversity capability at the receiver end helps in reducing the required energy per information to noise power spectral density (Eb/No) ratio at the receiver side. Typically, the diversity gain amounts up to 3 db both on the UE side as well as the eNodeB receiver side.

Cable and Connector Losses

Typically, the cable and connector losses can amount to between 2 to 3 db, depending on the quality of the cables and connectors used.

Propagation Loss

Propagation loss accounts for the largest variable in the link budget calculation. The propagation loss depends on a number of factors such as carrier frequency, UE distance from the transmitter, terrain and clutter, antenna height and tilt, among others.

Path loss calculation is purely theoretical, and there are various propagation models that can be used to determine the path loss and, in turn, a cell radius for a particular site. Some of the popular propagation models are the Okumura-Hata model, free space model, irregular terrain model, Du Path loss model, and diffracting screens model.

To calculate the path loss for a dense urban site using the Okumura–Hata model, the following formula is used:

$$L = A + B \log_{10} f_c - 13.82 \log_{10} h_b - a(h_m) + [C - 6.55 \log_{10} h_b] . \log d$$,

where L is the Path loss in decibels, hB is the height of the antenna (eNodeB antenna) in meters, hm is the height of the UE antenna in meters, f is the carrier frequency in megahertz, d is the distance between the UE and eNodeB in kilometers, and A, B, and C are constants.

Table 1-1 is a sample RF link budget with various losses and gains on the transmitting and receiving sides.

Table 1-1. *Link Budget Parameters for the Transmitting and Receiving Entities*

	UPLINK	DOWNLINK
TRANSMITTING ENTITY	**UE**	**eNodeB**
Tx RF Output Power	23dBm	40dBM
Body Loss	3dB	0dB
Combiner Loss	0dB	0dB
Feeder Loss	0dB	1.5dB
Connector Loss	0dB	2dB
Tx Antenna Gain	0dB	17.5dB
EIRP	20dBm	54dBM
RECEIVING ENTITY	**eNodeB**	**UE**
Rx Sensitivity	-104dBm	-102dBm
Rx Antenna Gain	17.5dB	0dB
Diversity Gain	3dB	0dB
Connector Loss	2dB	0dB
Feeder Loss	1.5dB	0dB
Interference Degradation Margin	3dB	3dB
Body Loss	0dB	3dB
Duplexer Loss	0dB	0dB
Rx power	-118dBm	-96dBm
Fade Margin	4dB	4dB
Required Isotropic Power	-114dBm	-92dBm
Maximum Permissible Path Loss	134dB	146dB

With these parameters, a cell dimensioning is performed for 384 Kbps of data, assuming the Okumura–Hata propagation model in a dense urban area. The cell sizing is calculated as shown in Table 1-2.

Table 1-2. *Cell Range Calculation for 384 Kbps Data Rate Using the Okumara-Hata Path Loss Model*

Allowed Propagation Loss = 146 dB in DL and 134 db in UL		Unit
Carrier frequency	2300	MHz
BS antenna height	25	M
UE antenna height	1.5	M
Parameter A value	46.3	
Parameter B value	33.9	
Parameter C value	44.9	
UE antenna gain function	-0.00092	
Pathloss exponent	3.574349	
Pathloss constant	137.3351	Db
Downlink range	1.496663	Km
Uplink range	1.191201	Km
Cell range	**1.191201**	**Kms**
Site hexagon coverage area	**2.911**	**sq kms**

LTE Band

The Evolved Universal Terrestrial Radio Access (E-UTRA) band for frequency division duplex (FDD) and time division duplex (TDD) modes is provided in Table 1-3 as derived from 3GPP spec 36.104. It can be seen from the table that the range at which the LTE cell can operate is quite huge. Logically, every operator, if given a choice, would want to deploy their network with the E-UTRA band, which operates at a very low frequency, because the losses associated with lower frequencies are much less in comparison with higher frequency losses. This would have an impact on the cell size and, in turn, the coverage planning for an operator.

Table 1-3. *Operating Bands for 3GPP TS 36.104*

E-UTRA Operating Band	Uplink (UL) operating band BS receive UE transmit $F_{UL\_low} - F_{UL\_high}$	Downlink (DL) operating band BS transmit UE receive $F_{DL\_low} - F_{DL\_high}$	Duplex Mode
1	1920 MHz – 1980 MHz	2110 MHz – 2170 MHz	FDD
2	1850 MHz – 1910 MHz	1930 MHz – 1990 MHz	FDD
3	1710 MHz – 1785 MHz	1805 MHz – 1880 MHz	FDD
4	1710 MHz – 1755 MHz	2110 MHz – 2155 MHz	FDD
5	824 MHz – 849 MHz	869 MHz – 894 MHz	FDD
6	830 MHz – 840 MHz	875 MHz – 885 MHz	FDD
7	2500 MHz – 2570 MHz	2620 MHz – 2690 MHz	FDD
8	880 MHz – 915 MHz	925 MHz – 960 MHz	FDD
9	1749.9 MHz – 1784.9 MHz	1844.9 MHz – 1879.9 MHz	FDD
10	1710 MHz – 1770 MHz	2110 MHz – 2170 MHz	FDD
11	1427.9 MHz – 1447.9 MHz	1475.9 MHz – 1495.9 MHz	FDD
12	699 MHz – 716 MHz	729 MHz – 746 MHz	FDD
13	777 MHz – 787 MHz	746 MHz – 756 MHz	FDD
14	788 MHz – 798 MHz	758 MHz – 768 MHz	FDD
15	Reserved	Reserved	FDD
16	Reserved	Reserved	FDD
17	704 MHz – 716 MHz	734 MHz – 746 MHz	FDD
18	815 MHz – 830 MHz	860 MHz – 875 MHz	FDD
19	830 MHz – 845 MHz	875 MHz – 890 MHz	FDD
20	832 MHz – 862 MHz	791 MHz – 821 MHz	FDD
21	1447.9 MHz – 1462.9 MHz	1495.9 MHz – 1510.9 MHz	FDD
...			
23	2000 MHz – 2020 MHz	2180 MHz – 2200 MHz	FDD
24	1626.5 MHz – 1660.5 MHz	1525 MHz – 1559 MHz	FDD
25	1850 MHz – 1915 MHz	1930 MHz – 1995 MHz	FDD
...			
33	1900 MHz – 1920 MHz	1900 MHz – 1920 MHz	TDD
34	2010 MHz – 2025 MHz	2010 MHz – 2025 MHz	TDD
35	1850 MHz – 1910 MHz	1850 MHz – 1910 MHz	TDD
36	1930 MHz – 1990 MHz	1930 MHz – 1990 MHz	TDD

(continued)

Table 1-3. (*continued*)

E-UTRA Operating Band	Uplink (UL) operating band BS receive UE transmit $F_{UL\_low} - F_{UL\_high}$	Downlink (DL) operating band BS transmit UE receive $F_{DL\_low} - F_{DL\_high}$	Duplex Mode
37	1910 MHz – 1930 MHz	1910 MHz – 1930 MHz	TDD
38	2570 MHz – 2620 MHz	2570 MHz – 2620 MHz	TDD
39	1880 MHz – 1920 MHz	1880 MHz – 1920 MHz	TDD
40	2300 MHz – 2400 MHz	2300 MHz – 2400 MHz	TDD
41	2496 MHz – 2690 MHz	2496 MHz – 2690 MHz	TDD
42	3400 MHz – 3600 MHz	3400 MHz – 3600 MHz	TDD
43	3600 MHz – 3800 MHz	3600 MHz – 3800 MHz	TDD

Note 1: Band 6 is not applicable.

The bands are regulated in terms of the allowed operating bandwidth. This is driven largely by the amount of available spectrum in each of the bands. Band allocation is mainly based on the availability of the spectrum for LTE deployment. Also, the UEs will need to support these bands to be able to latch on to the network and, depending on the area of selling, the UEs are enabled for a particular set of LTE bands. For example, for North America, the bands that are reserved for deployment of LTE are bands 2, 4, 5, 7, 8, 10, 12, 13, 14, 17, 18, and 19. For China, the reserved bands are 1, 3, 34, 39, and 40.

Bandwidth Options

In LTE, as shown in Figure 1-4, there are multiple bandwidth options ranging from 1.4 to 20 MHz. In cases of carrier aggregation, multiple 20 MHz carriers are aggregated to obtain a higher bandwidth.

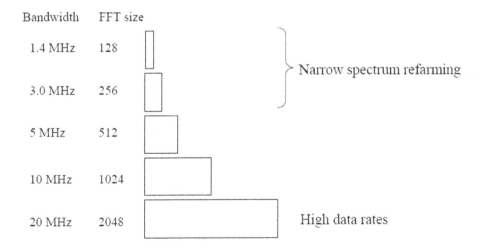

Figure 1-4. *Multiple bandwidth options*

Why is such a range of bandwidth required? The main target of operators using a lower bandwidth of 1.4 or 3.0 MHz is to perform spectral refarming, wherein the operator can maximize the global system for mobile communications (GSM) spectrum by refarming to LTE.

Operators can refarm using a much narrower spectrum than before and deliver GSM and wideband code division multiple access (WCDMA) with less spectrum and also lower total cost of ownership. Moreover, they can deliver a vastly improved user experience and potentially attract more customers to increase revenues.

Larger bandwidths of 10 MHz, 20 MHz, or more are used to provide higher data rates in a network.

TDD vs. FDD

This section compares TDD and FDD, and we will stick to the differences for these modes purely from an operational and implementation (deployment) point of view. However, the two modes of LTE have many more differences when compared from an architectural, designing, and testing point of view. A few differences that are seen between TDD and FDD are:

1. In LTE TDD mode, there is no concept of a paired spectrum. This also means that in any given instance, the eNodeB or the UE will be involved only in transmission or reception of the data, but never both.

2. For a TDD setup, the hardware design is much simpler, because at any given time, there is either transmission or reception happening, but not both. In other words, there is no need for a duplexer to have an isolated UL/DL path on the receiver/transmitter implementation for an LTE TDD device (UE/eNodeB). This also makes the equipment a little less expensive.

3. Because there is no difference in frequency for UL and DL for LTE TDD, the channel estimation or path loss calculation in both directions is similar. This eases the link budget planning activity. This also means that the channel estimation can be more robust in LTE TDD under load conditions and fast-fading conditions wherein the eNodeB need not always rely on UE reported channel feedback for corrective actions.

4. A large guard period is required for the eNodeB to switch from DL transmission to UL transmission. This results in a drop in efficiency and throughput for LTE TDD cell in comparison with an LTE FDD cell.

5. In LTE TDD, it is possible for 3GPP to allow different configurations that have a different mix of UL and DL subframes. Based on the traffic volume, the TDD configuration mode can be selected (i.e., for sites where higher usage of UL data is predicted, TDD config 0 can be configured whereas for sites where higher DL data are predicted, TDD mode 2 or 5 can be used). TDD config mode not only depends on the amount of UL and DL data but it also depends on the nature of traffic that is being used and the block error rate (BLER) history of the site. For example, if for a site the majority of the data are display sensitive, then a faster switching time (5 ms) is required, whereas if throughput and spectral efficiency are the criteria, then a switching time of 10 ms will be good. Similarly, for an area that is subject to very few retransmissions and higher DL data, TDD mode 5 would be ideal, whereas if the error rate is higher, then TDD mode 0, 1, or 2 would be preferred.

MIMO

This section will explain what MIMO is and the different transmission modes and advantages of each mode. The basic intent of this section is to explain the implication of MIMO on radio network planning and how or which MIMO settings can help for different deployment types.

Transmit Diversity Mode

In transmit diversity mode, each antenna transmits the same stream of data. At the receiver end, because there are multiple streams being received by multiple receivers, and the probability of reconstruction of the data is much higher, thereby improving the signal to noise ratio.

The transmit diversity mode of MIMO, if implemented in an area, will improve the coverage area by around a 3-db margin. The transmit diversity mode is useful for cells that are planned for rural areas where the cell size is typically large and users are typically spread across the cell.

Closed Loop Spatial Multiplexing

Closed loop spatial multiplexing is useful when the user's throughput or cell capacity needs to be improved in general. Because the closed loop spatial multiplexing mode of MIMO works on the feedback mechanism (Precoding Matrix Index [PMI] feedback) provided by the UE to the network, it is important that the UE is not fast moving and is either stationary or very slow moving for best results.

The urban small office model and dense urban model are two main deployment types where the cell can be configured for transmission mode 4 (TM4) (closed loop spatial multiplexing).

Open Loop Spatial Multiplexing

Open loop spatial multiplexing, like closed loop spatial multiplexing, is also targeted to improve the cell or sector throughput for a particular area of deployment. However, open loop spatial multiplexing does not rely on the PMI reporting from the UE but works on a predefined set of precoding selection for spatial multiplexing.

More often, the cyclic delay diversity (CDD) technique is used for open loop spatial multiplexing. In CDD, the transmitting unit adds cyclic time shifts and creates multipath transmission. The eNodeB tries to ensure that the transmission happens on the resource blocks for which the UE has reported better channel quality indicator (CQI) value. By doing this, the UE is able to receive the original stream as well as the delayed stream of data, and the delay on the transmit side ensures that there is no signal cancellation on the receiver side.

This is more useful for areas where the UE moves at a higher speed or the channel conditions change faster, for example, TM3 (open loop spatial multiplexing) can be set for cells that are modeled for highway deployment, which has many fast moving users.

Beamforming

Beamforming is a MIMO technique wherein the eNodeB transmitter tries to improve the quality of the signal that is received by specific users. This can be done by adjusting the tilt and power of the transmitter in the direction of the UE. Implementing beamforming can be very complicated, wherein the UE positioning has to be determined and the UE specific reference signals have to be configured for a cell. Also, the antenna calibration and maintaining the timing between the antennas will be quite challenging.

In practice, beamforming is useful for places where the cell geography is such that some users are in shadow areas and the only way to provide them with sufficient coverage is by beamforming.

UE Capabilities

Apart from the other factors discussed previously that can impact the LTE radio network planning and optimization, UE capability can also significantly influence the process of cell planning.

The cell throughput will depend on the average UE category within the area (i.e., if a site has higher distribution of category 4+ UEs, then the spectral efficiency for that cell will be higher).

Tables 1-4 and 1-5 are derived from 3GPP spec 36.306 and give an idea of the supported throughput for each category of UE in DL and UL.

Table 1-4. *UE Category vs. Downlink Throughput Support*

UE Category	Maximum number of DL-SCH transport block bits received within a TTI	Maximum number of bits of a DL-SCH transport block received within a TTI	Total number of soft channel bits	Maximum number of supported layers for spatial multiplexing in DL
Category 1	10296	10296	250368	1
Category 2	51024	51024	1237248	2
Category 3	102048	75376	1237248	2
Category 4	150752	75376	1827072	2
Category 5	299552	149776	3667200	4
Category 6	301504	149776 (4 layers) 75376 (2 layers)	3654144	2 or 4
Category 7	301504	149776 (4 layers) 75376 (2 layers)	3654144	2 or 4
Category 8	2998560	299856	35982720	8

Table 1-5. *UE Category vs. Uplink Throughput Support*

UE Category	Maximum number of UL-SCH transport block bits transmitted within a TTI	Maximum number of bits of an UL-SCH transport block transmitted within a TTI	Support for 64QAM in UL
Category 1	5160	5160	No
Category 2	25456	25456	No
Category 3	51024	51024	No
Category 4	51024	51024	No
Category 5	75376	75376	Yes
Category 6	51024	51024	No
Category 7	102048	51024	No
Category 8	1497760	149776	Yes

The UL MIMO capability of the UE will also impact the link budget calculation in the UL direction, as will the 4×4 MIMO support in the DL. However, in order for the planning to consider these inputs, it is important that a larger percentage of UEs in the area of deployment support these features.

Cell Sizes: Femto vs. Micro vs. Macro

Table 1-6 provides a brief estimate of the cell types, their usage, range, and the transmission power level that is typically used.

Table 1-6. *Different Cell Types and Use Cases*

Cell Type	Cell Range	Transmission Power and Other Characteristics
Macro cell	1 km to 100 kms	Transmission power = 10–20 watt port.
		Usually an outdoor deployment (e.g., rural deployment, dense urban deployment, etc.)
Micro cell	0.5 km to 1 km	Typical transmission power = 4 watt port.
		Usually an outdoor deployment (e.g., small office deployment, stadium deployment, etc.)
Femto cell	~500 m	Typical transmission power = <2 watt port.
		Ideal for indoor deployment.

LTE Performance Testing

Performance testing for LTE eNodeBs can broadly be classified into four test areas:

- Key performance indicator (KPI) verification
- Traffic model-based testing
- Overload testing
- Long-duration testing

To perform these tests, you must simulate traffic and generate load conditions with multiple UEs and simulate failures. Also, it is not possible to test all these cases as part of drive tests or field tests because some of these scenarios are not easy to re-create.

There are many tools available in the market that specifically target performance and load testing, such as Azimuth, TM500 (Aeroflex), ERCOM, and JDSU.

These tools are able to simulate multiple UEs performing different actions at the same time, and it is also possible to distribute the UEs at different distances from the cell center and simulate different fading models for these UEs (e.g., EPA, EVA, ETU, etc.).

It would be ideal to perform these testings with a performance test tool and then verify a subset of these tests again as part of a drive test or field test and match the results, so there will not be much difference between the lab results and the field results.

Key Performance Indicator Verification

The KPIs are very important aspects for any network element because they determine the need and the nature of optimization that will be required.

The 3GPP has standardized the areas for KPI validation in TS 32.425 as:

- Accessibility of KPI testing

- Retainability of KPI testing

- Integrity of KPI testing

- Availability of KPI testing

- Mobility of KPI testing

Accessibility of KPI Testing

Accessibility KPIs mainly determine how easy it is for the user to obtain service within specified tolerances and other given conditions.

The radio resource control (RRC) establishment success rate is a common KPI in this category. Other examples include paging congestion rate, RRC reestablishment success rate, RRC reconfiguration success rate, initial E-UTRAN radio access bearer (E-RAB) setup success rate, additional E-RAB setup success rate, among others.

In order to test accessibility KPI cases (i.e., the RRC establishment success rate), these considerations are required:

- The environment should consist of multiple UEs attempting RRC connections to move from the RRC_IDLE to the RRC_CONNECTED state.

- The UEs should attempt RRC connection setup at a higher rate of around 10 to 20 RRC connection setups per sector per second.

- In order to maintain a constant number of connected users per sector, it is also required to ensure a steady rate of users moving from the RRC_CONNECTED to the RRC_IDLE state per sector.

- At the end of the granularity period (which is known), the RRC establishment success rate KPI is derived using the following equation:

$$RRCS\_SR = \frac{RRCConnectionSuccess}{RRCConnectionAttempt} \times 100\%$$

- The tests can be repeated for different rates of RRC connection setups per second and for different load conditions (e.g., 30% load, 50% load, 70% load, 90% load, etc.).

Retainability of KPI Testing

Retainability KPIs target evaluation of how easy it is for a user to retain an established service within specified tolerances and other given conditions.

Examples for retainability KPIs are RRC abnormal release rate, E-RAB abnormal release rate, E-RAB release success rate, UE context release success rate, and average E-RAB number per active user.

In order to test retainability KPI cases, for instance, the UE context release success rate, these considerations will be required:

- Multiple UEs needs to initiate the attach procedure followed by a constant UL/DL data transfer procedure.

- For a fraction of these RRC_CONNECTED UEs, eNodeB should trigger the UE context release procedure due to user inactivity.

- For another fraction of the RRC_CONNECTED UEs, MME should initiate UE context release for various reasons (i.e., successful handover completion, handover cancellation completion, release of old UE-associated S1 connection, etc.).

- In order to maintain a steady number of attached users or sectors, new attached procedures must be maintained within the cell at the same rate at which UE context release requests or completions are maintained.

Integrity of KPI Testing

Examples for integrity KPIs are UL peak user throughput, DL peak user throughput, DL Internet provider (IP) latency, DL transport BLER, UL transport BLER, roundtrip time (RTT) latency, RTT packet loss (ping), among others.

In order to test integrity KPI cases, for instance, DL peak user throughput, these considerations will be required:

- A single UE should perform the attachment and should have at least one digital radio broadcasting (DRB) for non-guaranteed bit rate (GBR) data and one DRB for GBR data in the DL as well as UL direction for throughput tests.

- The aggregate maximum bit rate (AMBR) and the GBR values of the UE RABs should be sufficiently high (equal to or more than the cell throughput) and the application server that is connected to the evolved packet core (EPC) should be able to pump data for these RABs with a steady flow, wherein there is sufficient data scheduled for both of these RABs.

- The UE reported CQI should be maintained very high (around 15) to measure the peak throughput in DL for the user under ideal conditions.

- UE can be moved to the cell center, cell edge, and so forth, and throughputs can be measured accordingly for each of these conditions.

- The steps can be repeated for different propagation models (pedestrian fading, vehicular speed, etc.).

Availability of KPI Testing

For testing availability of the eNodeB, various tests can be run on the eNodeB continuously and the average downtime of eNodeB should be noted using the following equation:

Total testing time – eNodeB down time = eNodeB available time.

No special testing is specified to verify the availability KPI, instead the eNodeB downtime should be noted while performing all other performance testing and the KPI value should be derived.

Mobility of KPI Testing

Mobility KPI testing targets to verify the system performance during various handovers. Examples for mobility KPIs are intra-eNodeB handover success rate, intrafrequency handover success rate, interfrequency handover success rate, X2 handover success rate, S1 handover success rate, among others.

In most deployments, the handover is triggered based on the A3 event reported by the UE incase of intra- or interfrequency handover and B1 or B2 event reported by UE in case of interradio technology transfer (RAT) handover.

Events A3 and B1 are most often used to refer to a condition where the neighbor cell signal strength measurement is offset better than the serving cell signal strength.

In order to test mobility KPI cases, for instance, the intra-eNodeB handover success rate, these considerations will be required:

- Multiple UEs for multiple sectors are required to perform UE's attach procedure followed by a constant UL/DL data transfer procedure for each of these UEs.

- UE mobility should be enabled with different speeds so that the event A3/B1 is triggered for the UEs and handovers to the neighboring sectors are initiated.

- For a given sector under test, it is required to maintain a steady rate of outgoing handovers and an equal rate of incoming handover and observe the success ratio over a period of time.

- A3 and B1 parameters should be set to a different combination and consistency in KPI and should be observed.

- KPI should be monitored to be within an acceptable range.

- Tests can be repeated with inter-eNodeB over S1, X2, and interfrequency as well.

The KPIs should be monitored for different load conditions of the cell or eNodeB and will be repeated for different traffic profiles as well as different UE channel condition.

Table 1-7 provides a list of all KPIs for each category with targets for lab tests for most of these KPIs. Please note that these targets are assumptions and are based on some customer inputs and not necessarily a benchmark for pass/fail criteria for any of these tests. For integrity KPI cases, the target values will be different for TDD and FDD modes, and there can also be quite a bit of difference in lab test results vs. field results for these KPIs.

Table 1-7. *KPIs for Each Category*

KPI Category	KPI	Lab Test Target
Accessibility KPIs	Attach success rate	99%
	Detach success rate	99%
	RRC establishment success rate	99%
	RRC reconfiguration success rate	99%
	Initial E-RAB setup success rate	99%
	Additional E-RAB setup success rate	99%
	E-RAB setup success rate	99%
	E-RAB modify success rate	99%
	E-RAB blocking rate	<1%
	UE context establishment success rate	99%
	UE context modification success rate	99%
	S1-signal connection establishment success rate	99%
	Initial E-RAB accessibility	99%
	Additional E-RAB accessibility	99%
	Security mode success rate	99%
	Attach rate (attaches/second)	10
Retainability KPIs	RRC abnormal release rate	<1%
	E-RAB abnormal release rate	<1%
	E-RAB release success rate	99%
	UE context release success rate	99%
	Average E-RAB number per active user	2
Integrity KPIs	Single UE downlink IP peak throughput	
	Single UE uplink IP peak throughput	
	Single UE downlink IP average throughput	
	Single UE uplink IP average throughput	
	Overall downlink IP peak throughput	
	Overall uplink IP peak throughput	
	Overall downlink IP average throughput	
	Overall uplink IP average throughput	
	Single UE cell edge DL IP peak throughput	
	Single UE cell edge UL IP peak throughput	
	Single UE cell edge DL IP average throughput	
	Single UE cell edge UL IP average throughput	

(continued)

Table 1-7. (*continued*)

KPI Category	KPI	Lab Test Target
	Overall cell edge DL IP peak throughput	
	Overall cell edge UL IP peak throughput	
	Overall cell edge DL IP average throughput	
	Overall cell edge UL IP average throughput	
	End-end latency	
	eNodeB latency	
	State transition latency: Idle to Active	
	State transition latency: Sleep to Active	
	Paging latency	
	Downlink transport BLER	
	Uplink transport BLER	
Availability KPIs	Cell availability	5-7 weeks
Mobility KPIs	Success rate of intra-eNodeB outgoing handovers	95%
	Success rate of S1 inter-eNodeB outgoing handovers	95%
	Success rate of X2 inter-eNodeB outgoing handovers	95%
	Overall success rate of inter-eNodeB outgoing handovers	95%
	Preparation ratio of inter-eNodeB outgoing handovers	95%
	Success rates of outgoing handovers per cause	95%
	Outgoing handover failure rate	<5%
	Success rate of intrafrequency outgoing handovers	95%
	Success rate of interfrequency outgoing handovers with gap-assisted measurements	95%
	Success rate of interfrequency outgoing handovers with non-gap-assisted measurements	95%
	Success rate of outgoing handovers with DRX	95%
	Success rate of outgoing handovers without discontinuous reception (DRX)	95%
	Success rate of E-RAB establishment for incoming handovers	95%
	Outgoing handover cancellation rate	<5%
	Inter-RAT mobility	95%

Note 1: Details for each of these KPIs can be obtained by 3GPP spec TS32.425.

Note 2: The Lab test target for the integrity KPI can vary depending on the UE category used and the System configuration (2x2 MIMO, 4x4 MIMO etc) for e.g the peak DL throughput for a 4x2 MIMO FDD system should be greater than 140Mbps

Traffic Model Testing

As a part of traffic model-based performance testing, testing for different traffic models for different durations and KPIs should be observed for any variation or drop. Some of the common traffic models used or simulated are:

- Dense urban traffic model
- Urban small office model
- Urban residential area model
- Highway model
- Rural large cell model

Based on the traffic model, the parameters that are used for the simulation will assume different values (e.g., the number of users will be higher in the urban model compared with those for the rural model, whereas the speed of users will be higher in the highway model compared with the dense urban model). Also the usage of traffic will be different among these models.

The following sections present the parameters and their values that were used for a sample lab simulation of these traffic models.

Dense Urban Model

The number of users for this model will be higher (assuming around 150) for the first 20 minutes of simulation; however, toward the last 10 minutes of simulation, the total number of users will be gradually reduced but the total cell throughput will be maintained at 80% to verify the individual impact of signaling and user plane loading. Table 1-8 presents the parameters for the dense urban model.

Table 1-8. *Dense Urban Model Parameters*

Parameter	Values	Comment
Number of UEs	150	For dense urban simulation, the number of UEs at any given time will be on the higher side. The number of users should be derived based on the system load, which should be close to 80% for this traffic model.
User distribution	Uniform	For simplicity, we can assume user distribution to be uniform and user density to be high for an urban dense simulation.
Terminal speed	80% of the users are moving at 3 km/hour 20% of the users are stationary	We can assume all the UEs to be moving at 3 km/hour speed for this traffic model.

(continued)

Table 1-8. (*continued*)

Parameter	Values	Comment
Average number of sessions/ UE/busy hours (BH)	8	Based on data usage, traffic mix distribution from Sandvine, and application characteristics such as web page size, video duration. Low mobility users consume 50% more and high mobility users consume 50% less than the medium mobility users.
Number of E-RAB addition/ UE/BH	3	Based on the number of voice calls during the BH that would require one dedicated bearer setup. Low mobility users also make more calls than higher mobility users.
Number of E-RAB deletion/ UE/BH	3	Same assumption as above to remove the dedicated bearer.
Average session duration (sec)	300 sec	Based on the traffic mix and session duration per service type (e.g., streaming, browsing), assuming 25% longer session for low mobility user compared with medium mobility users. The difference could be viewed as low mobility users having a different traffic mix, which is heavier on video streaming. A similar assumption is made for the high mobility user in relation to the medium mobility user.
Number of attaches/minute	1	
Number of detaches/minute	1	
Data bandwidth (BW) consumption	8MB/user (including all the RABs)	Based on 1GB monthly consumption, 30 days per month, 5 BH per day, and 80% BW consumed during the BH. Low mobility users consume 50% more and high mobility users consume 50% less than the medium mobility users.
Number of tracking area updates (TAU)	75	Based on a periodic TAU of 1 hour or more considering that there will be 15 UEs in the network and the simulation will be for a period of 30 minutes, we can assume 75 TAUs for this traffic model.
Number of RRC reestablishments	2	Based on 1% Radio Link Failure (RLF) probability for medium mobility user and only connected users.
Data generation	Full buffer	For simplicity we can assume full buffer transmission for all the RABs
Indoor to outdoor ratio	1:6	There are different urban residential and urban small office and urban shopping mall models where the indoor to outdoor ratio is higher; in this model we assume that the traffic is mainly outdoor.
DL node B Transmitter-Receiver (Tx-Rx) scheme	2×2	MIMO is assumed for this traffic model.

(*continued*)

Table 1-8. (*continued*)

Parameter	Values	Comment
Simulation time	30 minutes	
RSRP quality distribution	Ratio of 30:30:40	The RSRP quality of distribution can be such that 30% of the users are experiencing excellent quality of signal, 30% of users are experiencing good quality of signal, and 40% of users are experiencing poor quality of signal. The reason for higher poor quality of signal is because the cell size for urban dense simulation will be smaller and many of the users will be toward the cell edge because they will be initiating a handover.
Number of incoming handovers	60	This can further be divided into the type of handover (S1/X2 handover).
Number of outgoing handovers	60	This can further be divided into the type of handover (S1/X2 handover).
Number of data sessions/ subscriber	2	

Urban Small Office Model

The main difference between the urban small office model and dense urban model will be the user distribution and the mobility of the users. In a small office model, the majority of the users will be stationary, and at the cell center, there will be a lesser number of handovers during busy hours.

The usage of traffic will be higher, but the number of users will be lower for this model compared with that of the dense urban model.

During the last 5 minutes of the simulation, you will need to simulate an inverse situation to that of the first 25 minutes wherein many cell center users will move toward the cell edge and handover to other cells and the traffic distribution will inverse from cell centric to cell edge and outward mobility.

Table 1-9 presents a list of parameters and the values for the urban small office traffic model.

Table 1-9. *Parameters for the Urban Small Office Traffic Model*

Parameter	Values	Comment
Number of UEs	80	For urban small office simulation, the number of UEs at any given time will be moderate and the system load for this kind of a setup is assumed to be around 85%.
User distribution	Concentrated at cell center and scattered and very low density toward the cell edge.	The user distribution will be dense in the cell center and scattered or uneven toward the cell edge. However, toward the last 5 minutes of simulation, the user distribution will be opposite wherein the cell center users who were stationary earlier now become mobile and move toward the cell edge and handover to the neighboring cell. Also the throughput for the cell will drop during the last 5 minutes of the simulation.
Terminal speed	80% of the users are stationary 10% of the users are moving at EPA (3 km/hr speed). 10% of the users are moving at around 30 kmph (vehicular speed).	
Average number of sessions/UE/busy hour (BH)	8	The assumption is that average duration of a session and the average number of sessions/users are both higher in a small office model.
Number of E-RAB addition/UE/BH	2	Based on the number of voice calls during the BH that would require one dedicated bearer setup. Low mobility users also make more calls than higher mobility users.
Number of E-RAB deletion/UE/BH	2	Same assumption as above to remove the dedicated bearer.
Average session duration (sec)	600 sec	The assumption is that the average duration of a session and the average number of sessions/users are both higher in a small office model.
Number of attaches/ minute	1	
Number of detaches/ minute	1	
Data bandwidth consumption	15 MB/user (including all the RABs)	Considering that the number of users who are stationary is around 80% and there is not much inward/outward mobility for the first 25 minutes of simulation, the average data consumption of a user will be higher.

(continued)

25

Table 1-9. (*continued*)

Parameter	Values	Comment
Number of TAUs	75	Based on a periodic TAU of 1 hour or more considering that there will be 15 UEs in the network and the simulation will be for a period of 30 minutes, we can assume 75 TAUs for this traffic model.
Number of RRC reestablishments	2	Based on 1% radio link failure (RLF) probability for medium mobility user and only connected users would experience RLF.
Data generation	Full buffer	For simplicity, we can assume full buffer transmission for all the RABs
Indoor to outdoor ratio	6:01	Considering that the area is that of an urban small office, we can assume that there are high numbers of indoor users compared with outdoor users.
DL node B Transmitter-Receiver (Tx-Rx) scheme	2×2	MIMO is assumed for this traffic model.
Simulation time	30 minutes	
RSRP quality distribution	Ratio of 70:20:10	The RSRP quality of distribution can be such that 70% of the users are experiencing excellent quality of signal, 20% of users are experiencing good quality of signal, and 10% of users are experiencing poor quality of signal. The reason for higher good quality of signal being most of the users will be stationary for this model and at cell center (if rightly planned).
Number of incoming handovers	20	This can further be divided into the type of handover (S1/X2 handover).
Number of outgoing handovers	20	This can further be divided into the type of handover (S1/X2 handover).
		Toward the last 5 minutes of simulation, the number will be higher as many of the stationary users will be mobile and moving outward.
Number of data sessions/ subscriber	2	

Urban Residential Area Model

The urban residential model will be more or less similar to the small office model wherein most of the users will be stationary and the volume of traffic used by users will be on the higher side. However, the main differences between the small office model and urban residential model will be:

- Users will be more uniformly distributed in the residential model and will not be concentrated at some areas and scattered over the rest of area.

- The change in traffic conditions during nonpeak hours will not be as drastic as in small office case; the number of handovers and mobility of users will not be very high.

Toward the last 10 minutes of the simulation period, a simulation will be triggered wherein the number of users will increase by around 30% and these users will be moving at a vehicular speed (30 kmph). The number of outgoing handovers will increase by around 30% during the first half of this period (5 minutes), and the number of incoming handovers will increase by 30% during the second half of this simulation (5 minutes).

Table 1-10 presents a list of parameters and the values for the urban residential traffic model.

Table 1-10. *Parameters for the Urban Residential Traffic Model*

Parameter	Values	Comment
Number of UEs	50 for the first 20 minutes and 65 during the last 10 minutes	For urban residential simulation, the number of UEs at any given time will be moderate and the system load for this kind of a setup is assumed to be around 70%. During the last 10 minutes, we assume that there will be 30% more users involved in outward mobility for the first 5 minutes and inward mobility toward the last 5 minutes, and the load in the network will vary accordingly.
User distribution	Fairly uniform	The user distribution will be uniform for a residential traffic model. However, in the last 10 minutes of simulation, the user distribution will involve 30% of users moving from cell center to cell edge in the first 5 minutes of the simulation and 30% of users moving from cell edge to cell center toward the last 5 minutes.
Terminal speed	70% of the users are stationary 10% of the users are moving at EPA (3 km/hr speed). 20% of the users are moving at around 30 kmph (vehicular speed).	
Average number of sessions/ UE/busy hour (BH)	4	The assumption is that the average duration of a session in a residential area will be higher and the average number of sessions/user will be lower.
Number of E-RAB addition/ UE/BH	2	Based on the number of voice calls during the BH, which would require one dedicated bearer setup. Low mobility users also make more calls than higher mobility users.
Number of E-RAB deletion UE/BH	2	Same assumption as above to remove the dedicated bearer.

(*continued*)

Table 1-10. (*continued*)

Parameter	Values	Comment
Average session duration (sec)	600 sec	The assumption is that the average duration of a session in a residential area will be higher and the average number of sessions/user will be lower.
Number of attaches/minute	1	
Number of detaches/minute	1	
Data bandwidth consumption	12MB/user (including all the RABs)	Considering that the percentage of users who are stationary is around 70% and there is not much inward/outward mobility for the first 20 minutes of simulation, the average data consumption of a user will be higher.
Number of TAUs	75	Based on a periodic TAU of 1 hour or more considering that there will be 15 UEs in the network and the simulation will be for a period of 30 minutes, we can assume 75 TAUs for this traffic model.
Number of RRC reestablishments	2	Based on 1% RLF probability for medium mobility user and only connected users would experience RLF.
Data generation	Full buffer	For simplicity we can assume full buffer transmission for all the RABs
Indoor to outdoor ratio	03:01	Considering residential area, the majority if users will be indoors.
DL node B Transmitter-Receiver (Tx-Rx) scheme	2X2	MIMO is assumed for this traffic model.
Simulation time	30 minutes	
RSRP quality distribution	Ratio of 50:30:20	The RSRP quality of distribution can be such that 50% of the users are experiencing excellent quality of signal, 30% of users are experiencing good quality of signal, and 20% of users are experiencing poor quality of signal. The reason for higher good quality of signal being most of the users will be stationary for this model and at cell center (if rightly planned).

(*continued*)

Table 1-10. (*continued*)

Parameter	Values	Comment
Number of incoming handovers	20	This can further be divided into the type of handover (S1/X2 handover).
		Toward the last 10 minutes of simulation, the number will be higher as many of the stationary users will be mobile and moving outward or inward.
Number of outgoing handovers	20	This can further be divided into the type of handover (S1/X2 handover). Toward the last 10 minutes of simulation, the number will be higher as many of the stationary users will be mobile and moving outward or inward.
Number of data sessions/ subscriber	2	

Highway Model

Simulation of a highway traffic model will require these considerations:

- The cell size should be considerably large.

- The average speed of a user will be high (around 70 to 100 kmph).

- The number of users will be lesser and the mobility of the users will be very high, with around 90% of the users involved in inward as well as outward mobility.

- It is possible that the cyclic prefix for the cells modeled around highway are of extended types as the cells are normally of larger size.

- User distribution is fairly uniform as the movement will be a particular direction on the highway.

Table 1-11 presents a list of parameters and the values for the highway traffic model.

Table 1-11. *Parameters for the Highway Traffic Model*

Parameter	Values	Comment
Number of UEs	20	For a highway model, the average number of UEs at a given time should be approximately 20 and the total throughput usage should be around 40% to 50%.
User distribution	Fairly uniform	The user distribution for a highway model should be fairly uniform as the users will be moving along a specific path.
Terminal speed	80% of the users are fast moving at a speed between 70 to 100 km per hour. 10% of the users are stationary 10% of users are slow moving at a speed of 3 kmph.	
Average number of session/ UE/busy hour (BH)	8	The assumption is that the average duration of a session in highway area will be lower and the average number of sessions per user will be higher because of mobility and higher RLF.
Number of E-RAB addition/ UE/BH	2	Based on the number of voice calls during the BH, which would require one dedicated bearer setup. Low mobility users also make more calls than higher mobility users.
Number of E-RAB Deletion/ UE/BH	2	Same assumption as above to remove the dedicated bearer.
Average session duration (sec)	180 sec	The assumption is that the average duration of a session in highway area will be lower and the average number of sessions per user will be higher because of mobility and higher RLF.
Number of attaches/minute	10	Higher number of attaches/detaches due to the mobility of users.
Number of detaches/minute	10	Higher number of attaches/detaches due to the mobility of users.
Data bandwidth consumption	4MB/user (including all the RABs)	Considering that the users are on high mobility, the channel conditions will not allow for higher data rate for these users and hence the data bandwidth consumption will be lower.

(*continued*)

Table 1-11. (*continued*)

Parameter	Values	Comment
Number of TAUs	75	Based on a periodic TAU of 1 hour or more considering that there will be 15 UEs in the network and the simulation will be for a period of 30 minutes, we can assume 75 TAUs for this traffic model.
Number of RRC reestablishments	2	Based on 1% RLF probability for medium mobility user and only connected users would experience RLF.
Data generation	Full buffer	For simplicity we can assume full buffer transmission for all the RABs
Indoor to outdoor ratio	1:10	Considering the traffic model is that of a highway, there must be a negligible number of indoor users in comparison with outdoor users.
DL node B Transmitter-Receiver (Tx-Rx) scheme	2×2	MIMO is assumed for this traffic model.
Simulation time	30 minutes	
RSRP quality distribution	Ratio of 20:20:60	The RSRP quality distribution will largely depend on the mobility of the users in this model; considering that 20% of users are stationary, we can assume around 20% of users to be in excellent RSRP conditions. Further assumption here is that at any given time there will be 20% of users in a good radio condition zone assuming that there are another 20% of users who are under slow-moving conditions. Remaining 60% of users will be under poor conditions assuming that they are moving fast.
Number of incoming handovers	20	This can further be divided into the type of handover (S1/X2 handover).
Number of outgoing handovers	20	This can further be divided into the type of handover (S1/X2 handover).
Number of data sessions/ subscriber	2	

Rural Large Cell Model

Simulation of a rural large cell traffic model will require the following considerations:

- The cell size should be considerably large with extended cyclic prefix due to the large cell (if possible).

- Number of users will be less and the mobility of the users will not be high.

- User distribution is uneven, with more users concentrated in a few places within the cell and no users in many other parts.

- Very low density of users and a higher number of outdoor users compared with indoor users, and because the cells are larger in size, the mobility ratio is low.

Table 1-12 presents a list of parameters and the values for the rural large cell model.

Table 1-12. *Parameter for the Rural Large Cell Model*

Parameter	Values	Comment
Number of UEs	40	For a rural model, the average number of UEs at a given time should be approximately 40, and the total throughput usage should be around 40% to 50%.
User distribution	Unevenly distributed with users concentrated in a few places and no users in other places.	The user distribution for a rural model should be random with higher number of users in some areas and no users or low users in some other areas.
Terminal speed	80% of the users are pedestrian model moving at 3 kmph speed. 10% of the users are stationary 10% of users are fast moving at a speed of around 70 kmph.	
Average number of sessions/UE/ busy hour (BH)	4	The assumption is that the average duration of a session in rural area will be lower and the average number of sessions/user will also be lower.
Number of E-RAB addition/UE/ BH	2	Based on the number of voice calls during the BH that would require one dedicated bearer setup. Low mobility users also make more calls than higher mobility users.
Number of E-RAB deletion/UE/BH	2	Same assumption as above to remove the dedicated bearer.
Average session duration (sec)	180 sec	The assumption is that the average duration of a session in rural area will be lower and the average number of sessions/user will also be lower.

(*continued*)

Table 1-12. (*continued*)

Parameter	Values	Comment
Number of attaches/minute	1	
Number of detaches/minute	1	
Data bandwidth consumption	4MB/user (including all the RABs)	Considering that the cell size is very high, the throughput consumption per user should be lower.
Number of TAUs	75	Based on a periodic TAU of 1 hour or more, considering that there will be 15 UEs in the network and the simulation will be for a period of 30 minutes, we can assume 75 TAUs for this traffic model.
Number of RRC reestablishments	2	Based on 1% RLF probability for medium mobility user and only connected users would experience RLF.
Data generation	Full buffer	For simplicity we can assume full buffer transmission for all the RABs.
Indoor to outdoor ratio	1:5	Considering that the area is that of a rural large cell, we can assume that there are high numbers of outdoor users compared with indoor users.
DL node B Transmitter-Receiver (Tx-Rx) scheme	2×2	MIMO is assumed for this traffic model.
Simulation time	30 minutes	
RSRP quality distribution	Ratio of 50:30:20	Because the cell is larger in size, most of the users should be in the excellent to good reception area compared with the cell edge region. Also because the traffic profile is that of a rural area, the number of obstructions in the path that can result in shadowing or fading are lower in number.
Number of incoming handovers	10	This can further be divided into the type of handover (S1/X2 handover).
Number of outgoing handovers	10	This can further be divided into the type of handover (S1/X2 handover).
Number of data sessions/subscriber	2	

For all the traffic models used for simulation, the user data distribution was assumed to be those presented in Table 1-13.

Table 1-13. *User Data Distribution by Traffic Model*

Type of Traffic	Total Traffic (%)
Streaming	50
Browsing	16
Social	11
Virtual private network (VPN)	10
Marketplace	5
Others including voice over Internet protocol (VoIP)	8
Total	100

UE simulation will be triggered using a performance simulation tool and channel conditions along with UE speed. Distribution can also be done using either the performance simulation tool or a channel emulator tool.

The eNodeB will be connected to the element management system (EMS) where the KPIs can be observed over the course of testing.

Overload and Capacity Testing

Overload and capacity testing can broadly be classified into two categories:

- Control plane overload and capacity testing.

- User plane overload and capacity testing.

Control Plane Overload and Capacity Testing

Control plane capacity and overload testing deal mainly with determining the signaling capacity of the eNodeB and estimating the signaling load.

Control plane overload and capacity testing will involve tests like:

- Maximum number of RRC connected UEs that can be supported by a sector without compromising the KPIs.

- Maximum number of RRC connected UEs that can be supported by an eNodeB without compromising on the KPIs.

- Maximum number of E-RABs (default plus dedicated) that can be supported by a sector without compromising the KPIs.

- Maximum number of E-RABs (default plus dedicated) that can be supported by an eNodeB without compromising the KPIs.

- Number of simultaneous attaches procedures (number of attach requests per second) that can be supported by the sector without compromising the KPI requirements.

- Number of incoming handovers that can be supported by the sector without compromising the KPIs.

For control plane capacity testing, a test setup similar to test setup 2 is essential. For example, to test the maximum number of attached UEs per sector, the following steps will be required:

- For the sector running on a no-load condition, perform a steady rate of UE attaches in steps of 32 attaches, 64 attaches, 96 attaches, 128 attaches, 156 attaches, 200 attaches, and so forth.

- Observe the success rate for KPIs and monitor the drop in success rate. Continue performing UE attaches until the success rate drops below an acceptable KPI threshold.

- In order to ensure that the attached UEs are not disconnected from the sector because of inactivity, maintain a steady UL/DL data rate for each of these attached UEs.

- Note the number of attached UEs after which the attach success rate starts to drop below an acceptable limit. This would be used as the maximum number of attached UEs per sector.

- Try attaches with different rates (30 attaches/second, 50 attaches/second) and also under different channel fading models such as the EPA, EVA, and ETU models.

User Plane Overload and Capacity Testing

User plane overload and capacity testing will deal mainly with data throughput capacity of the eNodeB. User plane overload testing will involve tests like:

- Maximum throughput that can be supported by a sector for MIMO users under ideal radio conditions.

- Maximum throughput that can be supported by an eNodeB for MIMO users under ideal radio conditions.

- Number of users that can be scheduled by a cell for each transmission time interval (TTI).

- Tests to verify the GBR share/sector.

- Tests to verify the n-GBR share/sector.

Apart from these tests, the following tests also need to be performed under overload and capacity testing category:

- Memory consumption tests for different loads (no UE attaches, 32 UE attaches, 64 UE attaches, etc.).

- Computer processing unit (CPU) load consumption tests.

- Configuration of thresholds 1, 2, 3, and 4.

- Tests to load the eNodeB or sector to exceed threshold 1 and verify the actions that are triggered by eNodeB/sector to bring the CPU load below the threshold.

- Tests to load the eNodeB/sector to exceed threshold 2 and verify the actions that are triggered by eNodeB/sector to bring the CPU load below the threshold.

- Tests to load the eNodeB/sector to exceed threshold 3 and verify the actions that are triggered by eNodeB/sector to bring the CPU load below the threshold.

- Tests to load the eNodeB/sector to exceed threshold 4 and verify the actions that are triggered by eNodeB/sector to bring the CPU load below the threshold.

Long Duration Testing

Long duration tests are mainly stability tests, wherein the eNodeB/sector will be tested with calls that last for 48 to 72 hours. Some of the tests that fall under this category are:

- Single UE with UL/DL non-GBR data without any mobility and no change in channel condition observed for 72 hours (full throughput test).

- Single UE with UL/DL GBR data without any mobility and no change in channel condition observed for 72 hours.

- Single UE with UL/DL non-GBR moving at 3 kmph speed in a circle for 48 hours.

- Multiple stationary UEs with data transmission or reception of similar QoS class identifier (QCI) observed for 72 hours.

- Stability tests for UE using TM4 for DL transmission.

- Stability tests for a mix of UEs working under different transmission modes and engaged in data.

An application server integrated with Iperf will be required to simulate constant UL/DL data at a desired rate.

For multiple UE simulations, simulation tools can be used, and for simulation of UE speed and fading to test stability at different modulations, channel emulators can be used between the UE and the sector under test.

EMS should be connected to the eNodeB to observe and monitor the KPIs. CPU load and memory consumption should be monitored as well during the course of the test.

Summary

This chapter covered the various phases in radio network planning, the parameters that can impact the different phases of planning, the essence of capacity and coverage planning, the various modes of deployment, and verification tests and steps for a deployment that a specialist should perform. Most of these topics are technology independent (i.e., the steps and goals would remain similar irrespective of 2G, 3G, or 4G deployment), however, the targets, especially in terms of KPIs, will be different because the throughput KPI targets in LTE will be much larger in comparison with the targets in 3G.

The following chapter will introduce you to the concept of a Self-organizing Network along with a detailed overview of its architecture, major aspects and features.

CHAPTER 2

Self-Organizing Networks in LTE Deployment

This chapter is an introduction to self-organizing networks (SON). We will start with a brief introduction to the current network, its practical limitations, and the advantages of SON in the current network. We will then proceed with a discussion of SON architecture wherein we will explain the different types of SON, such as centralized, distributed, and hybrid, along with their advantages and disadvantages. We will then briefly discuss the different phases of SON and what activities are performed in these phases, and finally we will detail some of the SON features specific to LTE like automatic eNodeB setup, automatic physical cell identification (PCID) allocation, automatic neighbor relation, random access channel (RACH) optimization, mobility robustness optimization (MRO), and intercell interference coordination (ICIC) and explain the concept, design, and implementation of these features.

Introduction to Self-organizing Networks

In today's network, the activity of installation, deployment, and maintenance of a radio access network involves very high costs, especially considering the number of nodes that require deployment and maintenance. Also because of the dynamics of radio and traffic conditions, it becomes a very tedious task to be able to change the network settings to cater to these dynamics.

A self-organizing network is often used to categorize a cellular network for which the tasks of configuring, operating, and optimizing are largely automated. It mainly targets to reduce operational expenses, improve operational efficiency, and enhance and maintain a gratifying user experience, even under adverse conditions.

SON features can markedly improve the user experience by optimizing the network automatically and rapidly mitigating outages as they occur. This is an extremely important characteristic for all network operators because time to operation and time to repair are critical factors for an efficient and well-managed network. By embracing the SON procedures and algorithms, operators will be able to use these capabilities significantly to their advantage. This chapter discusses the various SON features, how they are able to overcome the current issues, and how they benefit the operators when deployed.

SON Architecture

With LTE maturing and an increase in the demand for capacity, it has become crucial for the optimal use of all network resources to achieve higher end-user experiences and better revenue from the available resources. For any self-optimizations to take effect, some optimization algorithms are needed to drive the self-optimizations.

Based on the implementation and deployment, SONs can be classified as:

- Centralized SON
- Distributed SON
- Hybrid SON

Centralized SON

Centralized SON, as the name suggests, consists of a centrally located SON framework. In other words, the optimization algorithms take place in the Operations, administration and management (OAM) system.

One main advantage of this kind of solution is that the SON functionality will be centralized and will be at a higher level, thereby being more use-case driven. The flip side of this solution is that the decisions are not as fast as the distributed SON type. Figure 2-1 presents a flowchart for the centralized SON architecture.

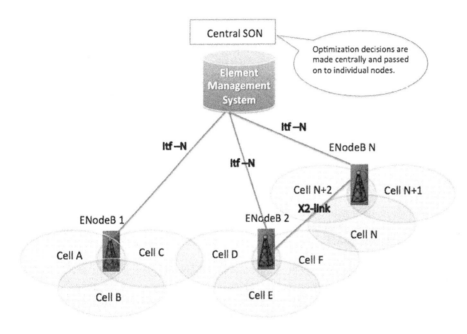

Figure 2-1. *Centralized SON architecture*

In centralized SON, all SON functions are located in the element management or network management level, making it easier to deploy. However, multivendor integration for the optimization of a solution can be quite challenging, as there is no standard driven optimization procedure, and vendors can have the centralized SON implementation suited to their network element.

A centralized SON solution is a preferred SON solution for optimization solutions that may impact the functioning of more than one network element. Optimization results can be stored in a configuration database and, upon completion, can be automatically distributed toward the impacted eNodeBs (network elements).

However, centralized SON restricts the possibility of quicker optimizations and SON adaptation, as there will be lag time in the network elements reporting the problem to the element manager and the central SON server applying the optimization algorithms.

Many vendors have a common optimization for simultaneous operation across multiple radio technologies. This can be a huge advantage, wherein joint optimization of LTE and GSM or WCDMA will be possible in an efficient way for these vendors.

A centralized solution is preferred for the following LTE optimization features:

- Physical cell identity management

- Neighbor cell relation optimization

- Interference reduction optimization

- Coverage and capacity optimization

- Handover optimization and load balancing optimization

- Radio optimizations, like RACH optimization

Distributed SON

In distributed SON, the optimization algorithms reside not at the network or element management system level, but at the network element level (i.e., eNodeB). The SON functionality and the optimization algorithm are not necessarily at a high level but can reside in many locations or network elements (e.g., eNodeB). This makes the deployment and optimization activities quite complex, especially when there is a requirement for multiple network elements to coordinate with one another as part of a solution.

However, for simpler cases with two or fewer network elements being impacted, it is more effective to approach this optimization or solution with a distributed SON model. Because the distributed SON solution resides at a relatively low level, the optimization algorithms can be executed much faster when compared with that for the centralized SON. Figure 2-2 presents a flowchart for the distributed SON.

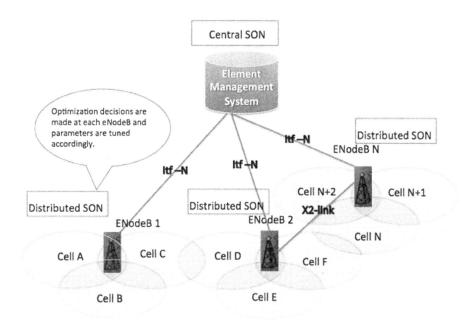

Figure 2-2. *Distributed SON example*

A distributed SON solution is preferred for the following LTE optimization features:

- Mobility robustness optimization

- Scheduler optimization for spectral efficiency vs. cell edge user throughput

The reason that distributed SON is preferred for these features is because these optimizations do not impact the other cells in the network and would only optimize the cell or eNodeB to improve the KPIs of the cell. Also, the adaptations can be much faster when these optimization parameters exist on the distributed level.

Hybrid SON

Hybrid SON is a combination of centralized SON and distributed SON, wherein a part of the optimization algorithms is centrally located and another part exists at the element or nodal level in eNodeB. In hybrid SON, normally at the distributed level, algorithms and optimization schemes that exist are targeted to provide a quicker solution, whereas a detailed, well-educated solution algorithm normally resides on the centralized level. This kind of hybrid solution provides more flexibility to the network over that of a purely centralized or purely distributed SON solution, thereby making it practical for different types of optimizations. Figure 2-3 presents the flowchart for the hybrid SON.

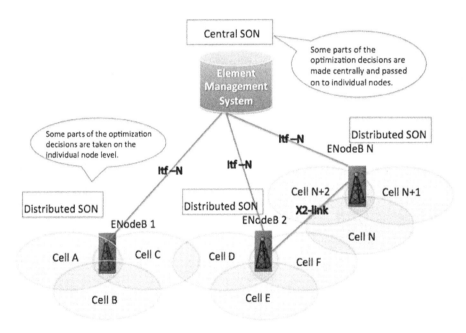

Figure 2-3. *Hybrid SON example*

A hybrid SON solution is preferred for the following LTE optimization features:

- Enhanced intercell interference coordination

- PCID collision or confusion detection

The SON deployment activities can be grouped into several phases, as described in the sections that follow.

Planning and Provisioning Phase

The planning phase of the SON is the phase wherein the operator decides first on the area for deployment. Depending on the coverage and capacity requirements, network planning needs to be performed. A planning tool is used extensively to create a network configuration and plans for the location for each of the network elements within the planned area to meet the capacity and coverage targets.

Parameter planning is also part of this phase wherein the parameter settings for the eNodeBs are planned beforehand. Typically the parameters that need to be planned in this stage are the transmit power, antenna tilt, handover-related settings, and Tier-1 neighbor list. The PCID and root sequence index planning are also performed in the planning phase.

Another important aspect of the planning phase is the transport network configuration planning, which enables the eNodeB to establish a link with other network elements like MME, neighboring eNodeBs, among others.

Commissioning and Operation Phase

This phase involves tasks like plug-and-play commissioning, during which the eNodeB automatically detects the hardware inventory by performing self-tests and brings itself up in an automatic manner. Upon bringing itself up, the eNodeB is able to download the new or upgraded software from a central location.

Another important activity that is performed in this phase is the establishment of links with peer entities like MME or neighboring eNodeBs. During this phase, the eNodeB also performs automatic configuration by downloading some of the parameters from the central SON entity. More details on these processes are provided later in the chapter.

Optimization Phase

The optimization phase is a continuously ongoing phase wherein the eNodeB as well as the central SON entity monitor the performance of the network element for various aspects like throughput, handover success rate, CPU utilization or load, and so on and performs optimization tasks to improve these KPIs.

Some of the key optimization tasks that are performed in this phase are:

- Mobility optimization, wherein the handover parameters are fine tuned to improve the handover success rate.

- RACH optimization, wherein the RACH parameters such as PRACH Config Index, frequencyOffset, and so forth are fine tuned to improve the RACH success rate and thereby improve the accessibility KPI.

- Scheduler parameter optimization, wherein the spectral efficiency and user experienced throughput are improved.

- Load balancing, wherein the cell suffering from high load and high usage is identified in the network and corrective actions such as diverting the traffic to a relatively low-loaded cell and so forth are taken to improve the overall situation.

The following sections present more detail on some of the features activated in these different phases of deployment.

SON Features

Broadly, SON features can be classified into three categories:

- Self-planning features
- Self-optimization features
- Self-healing features

Each will be discussed in the following sections.

Self-planning Features

Self-planning features are mainly targeted to reduce the initial deployment and installation costs. Features like automatic cell planning, automatic eNodeB setup, PCID planning, and automatic neighbor relation planning are grouped under this category.

Self-optimization Features

Self-optimization features continuously monitor the network performance, identify the problem areas, and then apply an optimization algorithm to improve the KPIs and the network performance accordingly. Some of the features that fall under this category are MRO, ICIC, and RACH optimization.

Self-healing Features

Self-healing features identify if there are any network elements or components that are down due to failure in a network and apply techniques to compensate for the performance degradation. They also automatically and remotely bring up the affected component. Features like cell outage compensation and load balancing fall under this category.

The following sections discuss in details some of the SON features from the different categories and explain how they are designed and implemented.

Automatic e-NodeB Setup

A major part of the capital expenditure (CAPEX) for an operator, apart from the equipment hardware and spectrum costs, is the deployment cost for the network. Deployment of an LTE radio network can be a very demanding and challenging activity and can involve subtasks such as:

- Network planning
- Hardware and software commissioning or implementation
- Integrating the network elements in the hybrid or multivendor environment
- Optimizing the network elements according to the field results
- Maintenance and support

For a complex deployment scenario, these deployment activities can cost more than the hardware and software costs. Therefore, it is very important that the complexity and cost of deployment are reduced and optimized as much as possible.

When it comes to the deployment of a network element, the integration and configuration of a network element are the most time-consuming parts of the process, and in most cases these are performed manually. Automatic eNodeB setup is a SON feature that aims to reduce the manual intervention for an eNodeB setup and commission as much as possible. This would also mean that the skill set requirement for the person who physically installs the eNodeB is minimal, thereby bringing down the cost of deployment. Also, because there is less human interfacing with the commissioning or bring up for the eNodeB, automatic eNodeB setup is less prone to human error.

Automatic eNodeB setup will mainly involve the network management system as well as the network element configurations. Steps for implementing an automated eNodeB bring up will involve:

1. *An automated self-test and self-discovery.* This will involve eNodeB identifying the backhaul and management links that are connected to it. Also, the base band unit and the remote radio head unit will need to be able to detect and identify each other in this step so they can communicate within it.

2. *IP assignment.* IP planning is done as part of preplanning, and the IP assignment can be done using a local console or dynamic host configuration protocol (DHCP). Here, the IP address assignment is not only for the new node, but also for the other connections that are configured, such as IP addresses for the Mobility Management Entitiy (MME), Serving gateway (SGW), other neighboring eNodeBs, and so forth.

3. *Automatic software management.* Once the secure tunnels are established with the EMS, the eNodeB will attempt to download the software from the central repository. Automatic software management involves centrally maintaining (at the element management system level) the software versions that are used in individual network elements (eNodeB in this case), keeping track of the latest available software, and scheduling the upgrade for individual eNodeBs. Typically, an eNodeB will have a base band unit (BBU) and remote radio head (RRH) as its two main components, and there would be separate software versions maintained for these two units. Management is required for each software component separately. Automatic software management will also require the element management system to support preplanning software loads for newly commissioned eNodeBs and provision a default image for these eNodeBs. Another important aspect of automatic software management is support for a "backup" and "rollback." In cases of unsuccessful upgrade events, there should be a possibility for a rollback to the previous version of the software.

4. *Automatic configuration.* Automatic configuration refers to the process by which the eNodeB configuration parameters are derived by the newly commissioned eNodeB. Automatic configuration is not restricted to only newly installed eNodeBs and can be performed on eNodeBs at any time based on the decision at the central SON level (element management system level). A system configuration file can be downloaded by the eNodeB from a central repository and should be locally stored inside the eNodeB for any rollback possibilities in the future. It should also be possible for the operator to push the configuration file to the eNodeB anytime on an as-needed basis. Some of the parameters that can be passed to each eNodeB as a part of automatic configuration are:

   - Individual cell's neighbor list

   - Tracking area

   - Individual cell's radio parameters, such as antenna tilt, power, and so forth

   - PCIDs for each cell

   - Any preconfigurations pertaining to interference cancellations (like frequency restrictions)

   - Root sequence index

- Handover-related settings (frequency offset, cell individual offsets for each neighbor, hysteresis, etc.)

- Blacklist or whitelist cells

- Transmission mode (transmit diversity or spatial multiplexing)

5. *Automatic inventory management.* Automatic inventory management enables the element management system to collect and maintain information about the components within the eNodeBs in an automated manner. Typically the inventory data will consist of:

- Serial number and other manufacturing information

- Identification of all field replaceable units

- Firmware and component inventories

- All software inventories

- Typically, the inventory information is uploaded to the network element in an automated manner and will be looked up during the these events:

  - When an eNodeB is initially commissioned

  - When a change is made to the eNodeB

  - When an operator needs this information

6. *Automatic interface setup.* This step would involve the eNodeB in performing S1 setup with the configured MME and X2 setups with its neighbors. Upon success of these setups, it informs the element management system about its operational state.

PCID Allocation

Every cell in the network must be assigned one of 504 physical-layer cell identity (PCID) values (0-503). PCID values can be reused as long as no conflicts exist. The PCID assignment function automatically assigns PCID values to enable a newly commissioned eNodeB.

The PCID allocation SON functionality should be able to support several high level functions, including:

- Initial assignment of temporary PCID values

- Transition to permanent PCID values following SON convergence

- Collision-free PCID value allocation procedure by the SON (i.e., the direct neighbors should not be using the same PCID values)

- Confusion-free PCID value allocation procedure by the SON (i.e., the PCID values of neighbors of direct neighbor cells must again not use the same PCID values)

- Avoidance of PCID group associations with PCID groups in use nearby

- Avoidance of PCID group affinity, preferring assigning three values that form a PCID group

- Avoidance of PCID sector uniqueness, preferring assigning three unique PCID sector values

- Avoidance of PCID sector alignment with antenna bearing, preferring PCID alignment with antenna direction

PCID allocation in a SON feature should also support collision and confusion detection and resolution.

Automatic PCID Assignment

Background

The PCID is a fundamental input for the physical layer, which implies potential radio interference if PCID assignment is not done carefully. As mentioned earlier, every cell in the system must be assigned one of 504 PCID values; therefore, PCID values will need to be reused in large systems. The automatic PCID assignment feature of SON removes the planning (reuse pattern) and provisioning issues from the process.

Common Ground

Initial PCID assignment provides the following capabilities:

- Operator can manually assign PCID values or use a planning tool

- Operator can choose to overwrite PCID values at any time

It is inevitable that some PCID conflicts will occur regardless of the initial PCID assignment solution (e.g., vendor boundaries, RF oddities). When PCID conflicts occur, they can be resolved with a distributed algorithm. To do conflict resolution, eNodeBs use their neighborhood data obtained via X2 for new PCID selection(s) and automatically resolve the conflict.

PCID Collision

PCID collision occurs when the eNodeB cell is using the same PCID value and frequency as another cell with a direct neighbor relationship. Figure 2-4 provides an example of PCID collision.

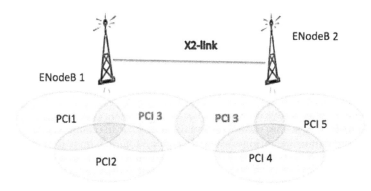

Figure 2-4. *Example of PCID collision*

This figure shows that the two neighboring eNodeBs, eNodeB1 and eNodeB2, both having cells with the same PCID (i.e., PCI3). This can be detected by the cells involved in PCID collision regardless of them being neighbors (i.e., both ends of a one-way relationship can detect it).

If two eNodeBs exchange PCIDs and the neighbor lists data via the X2 link, then both cells are in a position to detect and resolve the PCID conflict. A vendor-specific algorithm can determine how the conflict should be resolved. Some of the challenges in PCID conflict resolution may arise when:

1. An operator has chosen a fixed PCID value for a particular cell and SON algorithms are not allowed to override it.

2. An operator has chosen to disable the conflict resolution feature for SON.

3. There are no PCIDs available in the allocated range; this might result in a situation wherein no value would avoid PCID conflict.

PCID Confusion

When two or more cells on the same neighbor list are using the same PCID value and downlink frequency, it can result in PCID confusion. This condition can be detected at the cell that owns the neighbor list as well as at all of the neighbor cells that are using the same PCID value. Figure 2-5 shows an example of PCID confusion.

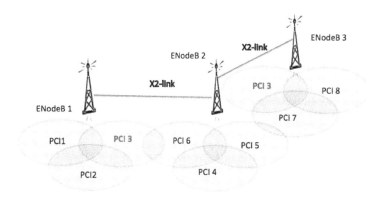

Figure 2-5. *Example of PCID confusion*

In this figure, eNodeB 1 sees that eNodeB 1 and eNodeB 3 have the same PCID (i.e., PCI 3). However, eNodeB 1 and eNodeB 3 do not have an X2 link and are not neighbors, so they cannot resolve the conflict. PCID confusion is detected by eNodeB 2, and it sends an eNodeB configuration update message with Neighbor Information IE (NI) filled appropriately to eNodeB 1 as well as eNodeB 3, which in turn would trigger conflict resolution based on its settings.

PCID confusion detection can also be a learned algorithm wherein the eNodeB detects the PCID confusion based on the UE measurement report. For example, consider Figure 2-5 where both eNodeB 1 and eNodeB 3 have a cell with PCI 3. Assuming that the eNodeB 2 is unaware of the cell with PCI 3 within eNodeB 1, if the UE measurement reports to the eNodeB 2 with PCI 3 as the only strongest cell, there is a good possibility that the handover will be initiated by eNodeB 2 toward the PCI 3, which is under eNodeB3. However, if the UE reports multiple strong cells in its reports (i.e., PCI 3 and PCI 2) the service cell can detect this as a possible PCID confusion case as the reported PCIDs according to the serving eNodeB belong to a completely different geographic location.

The eNodeB can further detect the exact cells and location of the cells that are under confusion by requesting the UE to report the E-UTRAN Cell Global ID (E-CGI) for the cells reported. In such cases, corrective actions can be taken to detect and resolve the PCID confusion. The resolution can be centralized wherein the eNodeB 2 reports the confusion to the central SON, and the central SON then perfoms a resolution act.

Automatic Neighbor Relation

In any mobile networks, including LTE, the mobility of the user equipment is usually guided by the network and based on the measurements that are reported by the UE for the neighboring cells. The UE is usually configured by the network to report the measurement for a set of neighboring cells based on various parameters such as:

- Geographic location of the neighboring cell

- Cell capabilities (e.g., does the neighboring cell support LTE technology? If yes, does it support LTE FDD or LTE TDD?)

- Neighboring cell relation with the serving cell (e.g., what type of link exists between the two cells—X2 link, S1 link, etc., and is the neighboring cell blacklisted, etc.)

- Priority of the neighbor (e.g., the operator might prefer an intra frequency cell over an inter frequency cell; in such cases, the neighboring configuration should be done accordingly)

It becomes very important for a cell to have a combination of static preplanned or commissioned neighbor allocation as well as a dynamic adaptive neighbor relation update based on the UE measurement reports and changes in the network to maintain flexibility within the network. Broadly, the neighbor relation management can be classified into two main steps: commissioned neighbor cell configurations and automatic neighbor relation updates.

Commissioned Neighbor Cell Configurations

This step deals with offline planning of the cells and its neighbors with the help of network planning tools. The operator may have minimal needs to plan for the IP addresses and the base station IDs or cell IDs for all the configured adjacent neighboring base stations or cells. The neighbor configuration can be static and does not require any assistance from the UE or other network elements.

During the startup of the base station, the commissioned parameters should be read, and X2 connections should be established to all the commissioned neighboring base stations. The remaining cell configuration information can be exchanged between the two base stations via the X2 link formed.

Typically, a single X2 connection is established between two base stations regardless of the number of supported cells for each of these base stations. This means all cells, each of them assigned with a unique global cell ID, have the same X2 IP address. If a newly deployed eNodeB has all the commissioning data, these will include the configuration data it runs from the X2 setup procedure to each configured neighbor.

When the connection could be established successfully (e.g., the listed neighbor is already installed and commissioned), all required neighbor information can be exchanged between the two eNodeBs. If a listed neighbor does not respond, it can be marked as not reachable.

When a base station in operational mode receives an X2 setup request from another base station, it typically should respond to the request, send its own cell configuration data, store the received configuration information in its own neighbor cell list, and mark it as reachable.

If the requesting base station for the X2 setup procedure is already known and neighbor configuration information is available with the target base station, the target base station can still send its own cell configuration to the initiation base station. The received information can then be compared with the existing ones and updated in cases of identified modifications.

Automatic Neighbor Relation Updates

This aspect is mainly 3GPP driven and is based on UE's measurement reporting. This means the UE detects the neighbor's signal strength and then reports to the serving cell with the PCID of the new cell. The serving cell is then based on these measurements, and it will add the newly discovered cell to its neighbor list.

However, the relationship between neighbor cells needs to be known by the respective base stations and should be planned accordingly because wrong configurations can result in a high rate of handover failures and call drops. Automatic neighbor relation updates can be broadly classified as a four-step procedure:

1. Neighbor cell detection

2. X2 configuration discovery of the neighboring site

3. The X2 connection setup

4. Neighbor relation optimization

Neighbor Cell Detection

An LTE cell can be identified in two ways. First, it is identified with the help of PCID, which is used for most of the RRC signaling, as it requires fewer bits for transmission. LTE cells can be identified and classified as neighbors based on the PCID; however, because there are only 504 possible PCIDs, there is a risk of a duplicate PCID being used by two different cells that are close to each other. The radio network planning and optimization engineers should ensure that for a particular coverage area, there are no two cells with the same PCIDs to avoid any conflicts. Second, the LTE cell can be identified with the help of E-UTRAN cell global ID (E-CGI) broadcasted as part of the SystemInformationBlock1, E-CGI is unique in the whole network and allows an unambiguous identification of a cell. Figure 2-6 shows the relation between the PCID and the E-CGI.

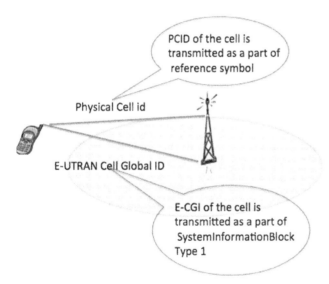

Figure 2-6. *Physical cell ID and E-UTRAN cell global ID*

During a UE attach, the eNodeB sends across the measurement configurations to the UE. When the UE moves away from the serving cell, it starts reporting measurements indicating the strongest cell or cells to the eNodeB for any handover-related actions. The measurement report consists of only the PCID of the cells that match the measurement criteria. In such events, it is very possible that the UE reports a PCID that is unknown to the source eNodeB. In this case, the base transceiver station BTS configures the UE to further report the E-CGI (E-UTRAN cell global ID) for the unknown PCID reported cell. Upon the UE reporting the E-CGI for the new target cell, the source eNodeB will try to derive the IP information for the newly discovered neighbor. Figure 2-7 depicts this process.

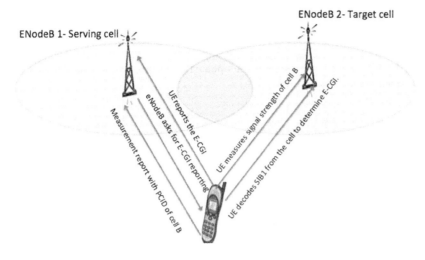

Figure 2-7. *Neighbor cell discovery*

X2 Configuration Discovery of the Neighboring Site

The E-CGI reported by the UE will now be used by the source eNodeB to discover the neighboring eNodeB. The source eNodeB will exchange the transport network layer (TNL) configurations with the target eNodeB via the MME by means of an information transfer procedure. Considering that the MME has already established the S1AP connections with the source and targeted eNodeBs individually, the eNodeBs can now exchange their configurations by means of transparent containers, as shown in Figure 2-8.

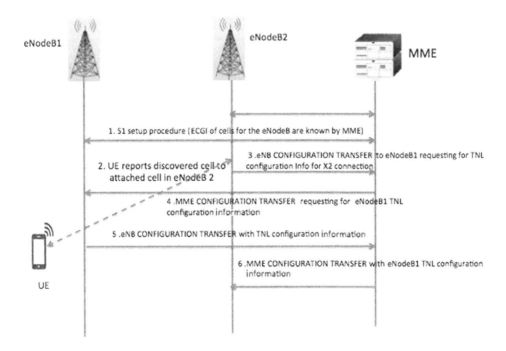

Figure 2-8. *IP address resolution procedure*

X2 Connection Setup with Neighbor Cell Configuration Updates

When the transport network layer configuration is received, the source eNodeB can then initiate an X2 connection setup with the target eNodeB. As a part of the X2 setup procedure, the two eNodeBs will exchange the list of serving cells with the respective eNodeBs. With this information, the eNodeBs can update the existing neighbor list with the new set of cells. The procedure is illustrated in Figure 2-9.

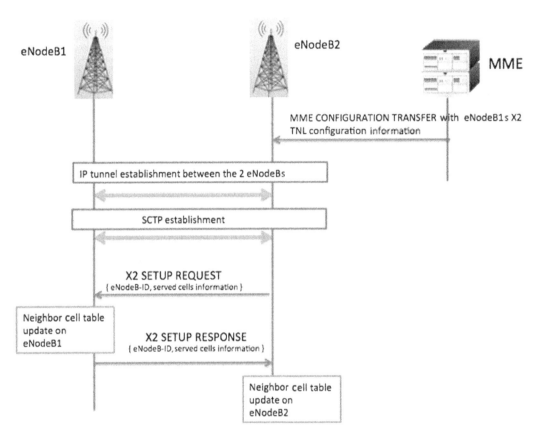

Figure 2-9. *X2 setup and exchange of configurations between the two eNodeBs*

Neighbor Relation Optimization

Broadly, there are two types of neighbor relations. First, there is a neighbor site relation, wherein there is a direct X2 connection existing between the two sites. In this case, the communication link between the two neighbors is known. Second, there is a neighbor cell relation, wherein the given two cells have a common or overlapping coverage area. UE always reposts a neighbor cell relation, but never a neighbor site relation, and only properly configured neighboring relations are relevant for handover performance figures. Figure 2-10 depicts these relations.

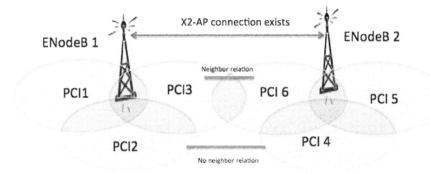

Figure 2-10. *Neighbor cell and site relations*

Referring to the example given in Figure 2-10:

- The eNodeB 1 has an X2 connection to the eNodeB 2 to neighbor site relation

- The eNodeB 2 parents three cells with PCIDs PCI 4, PCI 5, and PCI 6

- A neighbor cell relation exists only to the cell with PCID 6

When a new neighbor site relation is established, the configuration information of all parented cells is stored in the neighbor cell list. But only the identified and respectively measured neighbor cell is listed as a relation in the neighbor relation table (NRT) between one cell and a neighboring cell of this site.

During daily operation, a cell relation could fail to work properly for handovers (i.e., handover performance counters show higher failure rates than average). In this case, optimization algorithms can blacklist a relation.

Another possible optimization to the NRT is to mark the neighboring cells that are either under congestion or in temporary outage where handover is not allowed (shown by the field handover allowed in Figure 2-11). By doing this, the system information block (SIB) for the serving cell can be updated to avoid the cell information that is congested or blacklisted. The RRC connection setup and RRC connection reconfiguration messages sent by the serving cell to the UEs can be updated to remove measurement criteria for the cell. This information can also be used when UE reports measurement to the serving cell; if there are multiple reports from the UE, the serving cell can ignore the measurement report for the cell that is marked as handover not allowed and proceed with handover preparations for the other measured cells by the UE.

Neighbor Site and cell List for eNodeB 1				
Neighbour	PCID	E-CGI	Ip-address	Connection
	PCI6	ECGI1	172.168.10.1	X2
	PCI4	ECGI2	172.168.10.1	X2
eNodeB2	PCI5	ECGI3	172.168.10.1	X2
	PCI18	ECGI4	172.168.10.2	S1
eNodeB3	PCI19	ECGI5	172.168.10.2	S1
eNodeB4	PCI102	ECGI6	172.168.10.4	X2

Neighbor relation table on eNodeB1					
SI No	PCID	E-CGI	X2 Link	Handover Allowed	Priority
1	PCI6	ECGI1	Yes	Yes	1
2	102	ECGI2	Yes	Yes	2
3	231	ECGI3	Yes	Yes	3
4	34	ECGI4	No	No	6
5	45	ECGI5	No	Yes	5
6	501	ECGI6	Yes	No	4

Figure 2-11. *Neighbor site and cell list and neighbor relation table*

The NRT can be further optimized to improve the KPIs for a particular neighbor by adding an X2 link if there are too many handovers performed between the two cells or eNodeBs and there is no existing X2AP link between the two. Considering that the X2AP links that can be maintained by an eNodeB are often limited, there needs to be some mechanism for the eNodeB to decide on maintaining an X2 link with one eNodeB over another. One way to achieve this is for the eNodeB to maintain a priority tag against each neighbor in the NRT and update it at a predetermined interval based on the number of handovers performed between the two eNodeBs and the percentage of handover failure for the pair and the operator to which the neighboring eNodeB belongs. With this combination, the eNodeB should be able to use the X2 links only between high-priority neighbors and release the X2 link for the lower-priority neighbor. A sample NRT is shown in Figure 2-11 with some useful information for each of the neighbors.

SON and Self-Optimization Motivation of Intercell Interference Coordination

The LTE systems operate mainly with a reuse 1 factor, as this helps maximize the capacity and bandwidth usage. However, this also means that there is a very high scope of interference for the UEs that are at the cell edge. Depending on the measured signal strength from the neighboring cell at the cell edge, the interference can lead to a high performance or throughput loss for the cell edge users. In turn, this will lead to a drop in spectral efficiency for the entire network. Intercell interference coordination (ICIC) solutions try to bring balance between the cell throughput and cell edge users' data rate.

Principle of ICIC and Frequency Reuse

Frequency reuse is one of the best means to reduce intercell interference. The frequency reuse coefficient can be 1, 3 or 7. When the reuse coefficient equals 1 (i.e., adjacent cells are using the same frequency resource), at the cell edge, interference would be serious. A larger reuse coefficient can reduce intercell interference further, but care should be taken when doing this, as it will directly result in reduced spectral efficiency and cell throughput.

ICIC works on the principle wherein the frequency resource is divided into multiple frequency blocks (three blocks or seven blocks). Each cell will have a set of predefined physical resource blocks (PRBs) that are marked as cell center PRBs and another set of PRBs will be marked as cell edge PRBs.

Depending on the user location, a UE is either marked as a cell center UE or a cell edge UE, and the PRBs that are marked for cell center usage are provided to the cell center UEs. The PRBs that are marked for cell edge usage are provided to the cell edge UEs by the eNodeB scheduler.

Depending on the pattern of usage, care is taken to ensure that no two cells that are adjacent to each other will have the same set of PRBs marked as cell edge. Two UEs from neighboring cells (cell edge users) will not use the same set of PRBs, thereby reducing any interference to each other and improving the cell edge throughput. Figure 2-12 is an example of an ICIC deployment with a reuse coefficient pattern of 3.

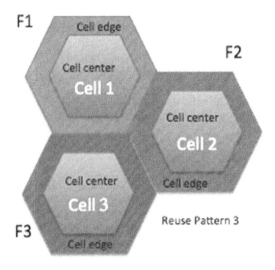

Figure 2-12. *ICIC deployment with a reuse coefficient pattern of 3*

ICIC may be of two types: static and dynamic.

- *Static* ICIC is a basic and simpler approach to implementing the ICIC feature. It is more suitable for cells that are predictable based on the type of traffic and the load distribution. In static ICIC, the parameters are configured during eNodeB commissioning itself. There are no reconfigurations and signaling with peers to negotiate on the resourcing pattern involved in static ICIC. Though it is a simpler approach, it is not necessarily efficient, as the planning does not always cover the different loading conditions and can result in performance degradation.

- *Dynamic* ICIC is a more complex approach based on the traffic conditions and cell loading. Dynamic ICIC is more suitable for cells where the cell loads a condition and the user distribution within the cell is not always predictable. Reconfigurations are typically triggered as part of dynamic ICIC to bring a balance between the cell edge user throughput experience vs. spectral efficiency. As part of dynamic ICIC, there are resource negotiations between the two eNodeBs via the X2 link as well. Though it is not as simple to implement the dynamic ICIC, it is more efficient and practical, as the cell sizes and the user distribution pattern in any network are not uniform.

Some of the key aspects that should be considered when designing and implementing ICIC with fractional frequency reuse mechanism are:

1. *Implementing fractional frequency reuse.* In the downlink, the fractional frequency reuse (FFR) scheme can be based on a preferred list of red, blue, greens (RBGs; color scheme). For each sector, its edge band consists of a subset of PRBs listed earlier in the list, and its center band consists of the remaining PRBs in the list. The common control channels of a given sector are assigned edge PRBs to the maximum extent possible to avoid overlapping with edge PRBs of neighboring sectors. Further, it could be made flexible by allowing the operator to configure the number of PRBs that are reserved for cell edge and cell center.

2. *Cell edge UE identification.* Considering the fact that the fractional frequency reuse design revolves around the PRB allocation for UEs ranged at different distances from the ENodeB, it becomes important that the UEs are classified as cell edge or cell center as accurately as possible for optimized results.

There can be different mechanisms used by different vendors to indentify the UE as a cell edge user. One of the most popular methods to determine or classify the UE as a cell edge user is based on the UE reported RSRP or RSRQ. Typically, there would be a configurable threshold value that can be set per the operator's requirement. When the reported or average RSRQ or RSRP value from the UE goes below the threshold value, the UE can be classified as a cell edge UE. Further, the bandwidth allocation for cell edge users can be either static or dynamic.

In static resource allocation, the frequency band for the cell edge users and cell center users are statically configured. In dynamic resource allocation, for each subframe, the target allocation bandwidth is determined by resource usage in past subframes.

When the system is less loaded, all users will be scheduled within the edge band only when the system is overloaded beyond a particular threshold. Edge users will be scheduled in the edge band, and center users will be scheduled in the center band.

RACH Optimization

In LTE, a random access procedure can be performed by user equipment under the following conditions:

1. IDLE user equipment performs an initial access procedure to move to the CONNECTED state.

2. User equipment performs a handover to a target cell.

3. When user equipment is in a CONNECTED state but out of time, synchronization occurs with the network, and it receives downlink data.

4. When a UE is in a CONNECTED state but out of time, synchronization occurs with the network, and it attempts to transmit uplink data.

5. When a UE performs reestablishment after it detects a radio link failure.

Need for RACH Optimization

In a homogenous network wherein the neighboring cells are using the same center frequency for uplink transmission, PRACH planning becomes very important and can very well be performed using self-optimization techniques.

User equipment that intends to move from an IDLE to a CONNECTED state to send or receive data will need to first perform a RANDOM ACCESS procedure.

The necessarily cell-specific RANDOM ACCESS procedural details are provided to the UE in `systemInformationBlockType2` (SIB2). Each of these broadcasted SIB2 parameters can be fine tuned or optimized by the network in order to:

1. *Optimize the balance between the RANDOM ACCESS opportunities and UL data transfer.* This is especially a concern in TDD modes of operation where there are not too many uplink opportunities for data transmissions, as well as RANDOM ACCESS procedures. During busy hours, when there are many users already connected to the cell and many more trying to connect to the cell by means of RANDOM ACCESS procedures, it becomes very important for the operator to be able to select the right base station setting for RANDOM ACCESS opportunities in order to balance the distribution of the uplink subframes between RANDOM ACCESS opportunities and user data transfer opportunity.

2. *Reduce interference during a RANDOM ACCESS procedure.* In a homogeneous network, where there are multiple cells deployed, there is a huge probability of uplink interference that can result in performance drops for the entire network. Care should be taken to ensure that the neighboring cells that are operating at the same frequency avoid using the same root sequence number. Also it is very important to ensure that the PRACH opportunities between the two neighboring cells are different and do not have RACH opportunities at the same time and frequency.

3. *Reduce call setup and handover delays.* This is extremely important in a deployment where there are users who are traveling at a higher speed.

The RACH optimization feature aims at automatically fine tuning the RACH parameters to enhance system performance. One of the targets listed in Table 2-1 should be used. Some of the performance targets that are configured by the operator as per the guidelines from 3GPP specs are outlined in the table.

Table 2-1. *Performance Targets from 3GPP Specifications*

Target Name	Definition	Legal Values
Access probability (AP)	The probability that the UE has for accessing the network after a certain number of random access attempts.	Cumulative Distribution Function (CDF) of access attempts
Access delay probability (ADP)	The probability of the delay that an UE can experience while accessing the RACH.	CDF of delays
RachOptAccessDelay Probability	This defines the list of ADPs that is acceptable.	ADPs are listed as a pair (a,b).
	For a sampling period of time, each entry in the ADP list defines the maximum time delay before an UE can access the random access channel with a specific success percentage.	An a in the list represents probability in percentages and a b represents the delay in ms.
	This target is suitable for RACH Optimization (RO)	If ADPx's a is larger than that of ADPy, then ADPx's b also has to be larger than the b of ADPy.

(continued)

Table 2-1. (*continued*)

Target Name	Definition	Legal Values
RachOptAccess Probability	This defines the list of Access Probability (APn) that is acceptable. Each instance of APn of the list is the probability that the UE gets access on the RACH within n number of attempts over an unspecified sampling period. For a sampling period, each entry in the APn list defines the probability of an UE to be able to access the RACH within n attempts. This target is suitable for RO.	APn's are listed as a pair (a, n). An a in the list represents probability in percentages and n represents the number of attempts. If APx's a is larger than that of APy, then APx's n has to be also larger than n of APy.
roSwitch	Indicates if the RACH optimization feature is activated or deactivated.	On, off

The parameters presented in Table 2-2 are broadcasted by a base station under SIB2 that corresponds to the PRACH characteristics.

Table 2-2. *PRACH Configuration Elements*

```
-- ASN1START

PRACH-ConfigSIB ::=              SEQUENCE {
      rootSequenceIndex              INTEGER (0..837),
      prach-ConfigInfo               PRACH-CinfigInfo
}

PRACH-Config ::=                 SEQUENCE {              OPTIONAL    -- Need ON
      rootSequenceIndex              INTEGER (0..837),
      prach-ConfigInfo               PRACH-CinfigInfo
}

PRACH-ConfigInfo ::=             SEQUENCE {
      prach-ConfigIndex              INTEGER (0..63)
      highSpeedFlag                  BOOLEAN,
      zeroCorrelationZoneConfig      INTEGER (0..15)
      prach-FreqOffset               INTEGER (0..94)
}
```

Prach-ConfigIndex

The parameter `Prach-ConfigIndex` provides the information about random access opportunities that are available in a particular sector of the UE. There are 64 possible values that a `Prach-ConfigIndex` can assume, and each value provides information about the network the UE can use to attempt random access:

- Preamble format of the PRACH used

- Number of PRACH opportunities

- System frames during which the PRACH opportunities are configured

- Subframes where the PRACH opportunities are configured by the network

The preamble format and parameters are shown in Figure 2-13.

CP	Sequence

T_{CP} T_{SEQ}

Random access preamble format

Random access preamble parameters

Preamble format	T_{CP}	T_{SEQ}
0	$3168 \cdot T_s$	$24576 \cdot T_s$
1	$21024 \cdot T_s$	$24576 \cdot T_s$
2	$6240 \cdot T_s$	$2 \cdot 24576 \cdot T_s$
3	$21024 \cdot T_s$	$2 \cdot 24576 \cdot T_s$
4*	$448 \cdot T_s$	$4096 \cdot T_s$

Figure 2-13. *Preamble format and paramters used for PRACH*

For an FDD deployment, the number of PRACH opportunities within a subframe cannot exceed 1. However, due to the shortage of uplink opportunities in the TDD network, there can be up to six PRACH opportunities. In order to reduce the call setup delays or handover delays, one of the parameters that can be optimized is the Prach-ConfigIndex, which can enable multiple PRACH opportunities for a UE wanting to establish connection.

Mobility Robustness Optimization

Mobility robustness optimization aims to improve system performance by optimizing the handover parameters. There are three popular reasons for handover failures for any LTE network: too early handover, too late handover, and handovers to a wrong cell. The mobility robustness optimization feature tries to optimize the cell offsets for two neighboring cells in order to reduce the failures that occur for these reasons. Optimization of these failures not only helps reduce the call drop ratio, but also significantly brings down the signaling load on a cell or eNodeB. Mobility robustness is part of the 3GPP's SON use cases (TR 36.902 V9.0.0).

During deployment, the operator defines a default set of configuration for the mobility parameters based on the type of deployment (e.g., urban, dense urban, small office, rural). This set of parameters (default parameterization) is not always optimal and might not yield the desired KPIs upon deployment. Mobility robustness features aim to target these cells that are not optimally configured to continuously improve the mobility parameters by fine tuning them until a desired result is obtained, hence improving the overall mobility performance. Detection of poor mobility performance is based on the long-term evaluation of certain mobility counters and KPIs.

The operator can further specify how mobility robustness should be fine tuned by being able to configure the trigger conditions and exit criteria for these triggers. Let's have a look at the types of handover failures, how they can be detected, and what actions can be taken for each of these failures.

Late Handovers

Late handovers often result in a radio link failure to the established connection even before a handover procedure is initiated on the source eNodeB side or the handover procedure is completed on the target eNodeB side. Often, in a late handover case, the UE tries to reestablish the radio links with the destination eNodeB upon radio link failure.

A popular means to reduce or have a check on the late handover failures is to detect such RRC reestablishment messages sent across from the UE to the target eNodeB and send them across an RLF indicator to the original source eNodeB. There the source eNodeB will recognize this as a late handover and can appropriately adjust the cell individual offset (CIO) for that particular neighbor so the percentage of late handovers is reduced for the cell pair. This mechanism is described in detail in Section 22.4.2 of TS 36.300-990. The RLF indicator message is described in Section 8.3.9 of TS 36.423-960.

For cases where the source and destination cell pairs belong to the same eNodeB, there will not be any X2 messaging to pass on the RLF indicator. Instead, the MRO corrective action will be taken care of by the eNodeB internally.

Figure 2-14 shows an example of how a late handover case is handled as part of the MRO solution.

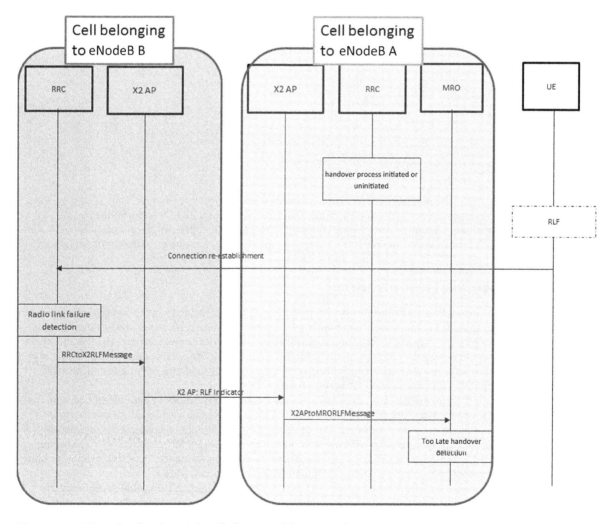

Figure 2-14. *How a late handover is handled as part of the MRO solution*

Early Handovers

Early handovers often result in a radio link failure for a UE that has been handed over to a target cell after handover is complete. Often in an early handover case, the UE tries to reestablish the radio links with the previous source eNodeB upon radio link failure.

A very popular means to reduce or check on early handover failures is to detect such RRC reestablishment messages sent across from the UE to the source eNodeB and then send across an RLF indicator to the target eNodeB where the radio link failure occurred. The target eNodeB then recognizes the UE as the one that was originally handed over from the same eNodeB and sends across a handover report message to the original source eNodeB, thereby indicating this as an early handover case. In the source eNodeB, upon detecting this case as an early handover case, appropriate adjustments to the CIO for that particular neighbor can be carried out so the percentage of late handovers is reduced for the cell pair. This mechanism is described in detail in Section 22.4.2 of TS 36.300-990. RLF indicator message and handover report message are described in Sections 8.3.9 and 8.3.10 of TS 36.423-960.

For cases where the source as well as the destination cell pairs belong to the same eNodeB, there will not be any X2 messaging to pass on the RLF indicator or the handover report. Instead, the MRO corrective action will be taken care of by the eNodeB internally.

Figure 2-15 shows an example of how a too early handover case is handled as a part of the MRO solution.

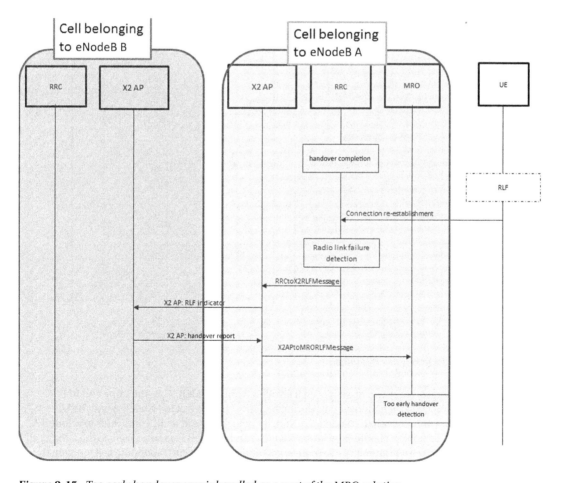

Figure 2-15. *Too early handover case is handled as a part of the MRO solution*

Handover to Wrong Cell

Handovers often result in a radio link failure for a UE immediately after being handed over to a target cell, followed by the UE trying to reestablish the radio link connection with a cell that was not involved in the handover procedure. For example, after a successful handover from the cell belonging to eNodeB A to a cell belonging to eNodeB B, RLF happens, and the UE attempts connection reestablishment in the cell belonging to eNodeB C (as shown in Figure 2-16). In this case, eNodeB C sends an RLF indicator message to eNB B, followed by eNodeB B sending across a handover report message to eNodeB A indicating handover to the wrong cell. This mechanism is described in Section 22.4.2 of TS 36.300-990.

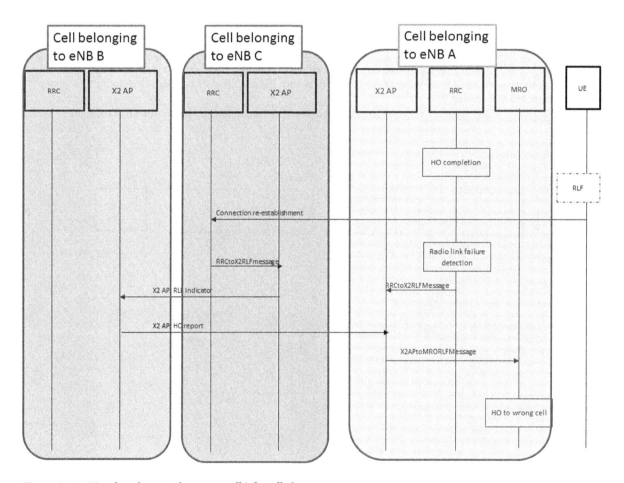

Figure 2-16. *How handover to the wrong cell is handled*

Note that the handover report message will be sent even if eNodeB B and eNodeB C are the same and RLF indication is internal to the eNodeB. Also, if handover fails during handover from a cell in eNodeB A and the UE attempts to reestablish the connection to a cell in eNodeB C, eNodeB C will then send an RLF indicator to eNodeB A.

In handover to a wrong cell, eNodeB A should note both eNodeB C and eNodeB B as handovers to the wrong cell CT (correct target) and handover to the wrong cell WT (wrong target) and adjust the corresponding cell individual offsets accordingly to reduce the rate of handover to wrong cell failure. Figure 2-16 shows an example case of how handover to the wrong cell case is handled as a part of the MRO solution.

Load Balancing

Clear load balancing strategy helps the multitechnology operator to optimize the use of their investments. Also, having a clear criteria for serving different types of traffic in certain network layer helps to ensure the capacity and service performance for mobile network subscribers. For these tasks, a centralized approach over the entire network area helps in minimizing the effort and time spent on load balancing.

Load balancing in LTE focuses mostly on air interface load balancing between different cells, between cells on the same of different frequency, and between different technology cells. Real-time load sharing is controlled with the handover triggering parameters and thresholds. The local optimization is based on real-time measurements.

There is also centralized support for load balancing in order to follow and ensure the adequate capacity in each network layer. Typically, the network management system collects the actual network statistics of load, handover, and cell performance and defines different criteria for these statistics based on the type of cell.

Typically, the central SON optimizer tool should be able to use the centralized information in other tools and analyze the load and handover performance against the actual parameters. The optimizer tool should be able to detect the cells continuously having high loads cells that are soon to reach the capacity limits and cells that experience the handover ping-pong effect and need optimization to improve the overall situation.

SON and Self-healing

Self-healing is one of the most important aspects of SON. There are various features that facilitate the self-healing aspect of SON, such as handover optimization, load balancing, cell outage detection and compensation, energy saving, among others. Each self-organization use case or feature involves fine tuning and optimizization of a set of parameters in a network element. The main goal for this parameter tuning is to enable self-configuration, self-optimization, and self-healing for the individual network elements or for the complete network as an entity. The main aim of self-healing is to detect a failure or outage and perform repair actions to recover the system from that outage or failure.

Let's look at an example case of cell outage detection with compensation to further explain the SON self-healing mechanism.

Cell Outage Detection

Cell outage is detected by means of various alarms and alarm correlations. The outage can be from a service, process, or the complete cell itself. The network element should be designed to raise alarms or report counters or KPIs corresponding to these outages and pass it on toward the element manager system (EMS) for further actions. At the central SON level, outage KPIs are continuously monitored. If KPIs are below threshold or if the alarms for the network element exist for an extended period of time, the cell is then marked on the outage list by the central SON.

Cell Outage Compensation

As part of outage compensation, the central SON will need to detect the best set of cells that can compensate for the cell outage. The compensating set for an outage cell can be predetermined by the central SON, wherein for each cell, an outage compensation is calculated prior to and upon outage detection, and these compensation algorithms are then executed. The downside of this method in outage compensation is that the compensation calculation is static and does not consider the current load condition of the compensating cells. Also in the case of multiple outages within the network, the predetermined cell outage compensation algorithm will be suboptimal.

Another way to compensate for the outage cell is to dynamically (upon outage) determine the best cells that should be used for compensation. Some of the considerations for candidate cell selection can be:

Proximity of the cell to the outage cell. Often the higher priority neighbors are selected as compensating cells as the amount of parameter tuning that will be required for these tier-1 neighbors will be comparitively lesser.

Current load condition of the candidate cell. As a result of cell outage compensation, it is very likely that after the compensation procedure is performed, the candidate cells will have a larger coverage area with an increase in the number of users that are served by it. Also the incoming handover ratio can increase for the cell because of the compensation procedure. Care should be taken to ensure that the candidate cells are not already under high load condition with poor KPI performance.

Type of the cell. Compensation algorithms will also consider the type of the candidate cell for any outage calculation (i.e., an indoor cell is not typically chosen as a candidate cell for compensation of an outdoor cell). Also, it is important that the candidate cell belongs to the same service provider so the impact to the revenue will be minimal.

The advantage of dynamically determining the candidate cells for compensation is that the estimation is more realistic and the risks are less as compared with that of static determination of the candidate cells. However, the time taken for the cell outage compensation will be much higher when performed dynamically.

As part of outage compensation, the parameters that are reconfigured on the candidate cells are typically cell mobility parameters, neighbor lists, cell transmit power, and antenna tilt. The tuning is performed in smaller steps and the KPIs are monitored for improvement. The action is stopped once the KPIs are in an acceptable range or the alarm for the outage is cleared.

Figure 2-17 presents a flowchart representing the cell outage compensation procedure for central SON.

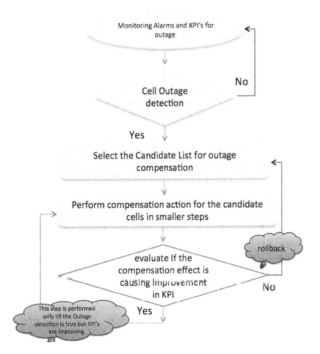

Figure 2-17. *Cell outage compensation procedure for central SON*

Benefit of Cell Outage Compensation

There are three advantages to cell outage compensation procedures:

- Minimizes the damage and downtime until the faulty cell is repaired.

- Repair activity can be postponed or planned, as the impact will not be that high due to cell outage compensation. This will result in reduced maintenance costs (e.g., no permanent on-call service, smaller stocks of spare parts, combining of trips).

- Cell outage compensation is extremely useful and critical in places where the frequency of faults is higher.

Summary

This chapter provided a brief introduction to SON and its benefits and provided an overview of SON and its architecture, deployment aspects, and some of its major features. The following chapter talks in length about the deployment, business, and economic challenges that the fourth generation of mobile telecommunications technology is surrounded by.

CHAPTER 3

■ ■ ■

Deployment Challenges in Evolving 4G

Experienced network operators will often agree that every deployment of any technology is a unique experience. Veteran players in the telecom field often have stories to swap when it comes to relating their experiences with the deployment of solutions in the field. For development organizations, design wins might indicate revenues to be enjoyed, but successful deployments are the real crowns to be worn with pride and bragged about in competitive environments.

So what it is about deployments that make them such celebrated events upon completion yet such daunting tasks to undertake? There are a variety of reasons for this. Many times, there tend to be problems inherent in the technology itself. The practical aspects of running a business in a highly competitive regulated environment like telecom lead to many other challenges.

A critical part of network and service planning rests upon user profiles (i.e., how the users and their usage patterns are projected). The changing nature of real-world users and their usage patterns pose a challenge. Applications and services that are used when designing a solution may become outdated by the time of deployment. Marginal services might gain some time in the lime light due to changes that cannot be foreseen, like the sudden popularity of some particular applications in the market or when new user equipment is introduced that seemingly increases traffic of a particular type. Being watchful for such applications is important, because usage profiles should definitely be taken into consideration when designing a solution.

This chapter will cover some of the traditional challenges that are encountered in LTE deployments when taking into account the nature of business, technology, and user equipment. We will then shift our focus toward traffic and user profiles. We also highlight some futuristic trends that would necessitate certain requirements of 4G solutions in these areas to help prepare for these types situations in a more efficient manner.

Technology-Related Challenges

LTE as a technology has been adopted widely around the world. Yet the issues presented here pretty much remain active and need to be taken into account for a practical assessment of deployment issues, even if they are only partially addressable in implementation solutions.

Interference Issues

LTE as a solution has been designed to improve capacity and provide higher speeds at better QoS. Higher capacity mostly equates to higher transmission power and places a lot of importance on power control so that cell edge users do not face too much interference. The farther the UE is from the eNodeB, the higher the power with which it needs to be transmitted. Also, even with the hierarchical layering of cells using different cell sizes (Macro, Pico, and Femto), interference still needs to be managed, both between the LTE cells and in an LTE cell (intracell interference) and with other radio access technologies that may exist (2G or 3G cells). Thus, intercell interference definitely increases in such scenarios. The tuning of such parameters in real time is even more difficult as environmental conditions vary during the day and the traffic patterns experienced by the eNodeB can also vary by the time of the day.

> ░ **Note** Interference issues and manual tuning for coverage and capacity are discussed in more detail in Chapter 1.

The LTE standards have provided for the intercell interference coordination (ICIC) as part of Rel 8 and an improved enhanced ICIC (eICIC) feature as part of Rel 10 for heterogenous networks. Implementing eICIC requires self-organized networks
to be implemented, including optimized algorithms to reduce interference. In a traditional macronetwork-based environment, ICIC improves interference only on traffic channels.

> ░ **Note** Enhanced ICIC is dealt with in more detail along with self-organizing networks in Chapter 2.

Spectrum Harmonization

LTE as a solution has been designed to work with multiple bandwidth options and multiple frequencies. LTE supports 31 operating bands for the paired spectrum (FDD) and 12 operating bands for the unpaired spectrum (TDD). Typically, the bands are allocated to specific frequencies, which are popular in specific countries, such as in the United States and Japan, to help with better acceptance.

Although the intention of supporting multiple bands and frequencies and providing for a wide range of supported bandwidths is to make an easier adoption of LTE with enough flexibility to support available bandwidth and frequencies, this definitely imposes problems for the seamless user experience that subscribers may tend to take for granted. A user with a GSM mobile, for example, could comfortably roam across the world without having to worry about compatibility and availability of services. A similar LTE user may not be able to do the same unless her phone supports the multiple bands as part of the services deployed by operators in such territories or countries.

We have already encountered issues of users purchasing LTE phones in some countries only to be surprised and disappointed that the same phone is not supported by the LTE services offered by the operators in their home countries or countries of travel. If standardization efforts are not able to narrow down and harmonize the frequencies to be supported across geographies, the onus then tends to fall on the UE manufacturers to support multiple bands. This may increase the cost of production and maintenance for the manufacturers and increase processing capacity, which, again, affects and imbalances the ecosystem. Higher UE costs may imply a larger barrier for user adoption and will also make it imperative to create business plans that will recover investments and work against operators' efforts to provide the best services possible at the lowest cost per user or serviced bit.

> ░ **Note** The cost per bit and other items like average revenue per user are discussed in more detail later in this chapter.

Voice Over LTE Implementation

In spite of the usage of data catching up with traditional voice offerings, as networks have evolved from 2G to 3G and LTE, voice still plays a prominent role in the product to be supported by an operator. Voice is of so much importance that LTE has evolved specific options and solutions to support it.

For those operators who want to optimize their networks for higher data performance and offload voice processing, there is the option of circuit-switched fallback (CSFB). In this solution, the operator hands the UE over to a 2G or 3G network to support voice, while suspending the active data connection with the LTE network. This implies that the operator needs to continue to support 2G and3G networks, including their legacy core network elements. Such solutions may not appeal to the service-conscious business user, for instance, who expects all services to be available without interruption all the time.

■ **Note**   See Chapter 1 for more details on the key KPIs defined by the Third Generation Partnership Project (3GPP) that need to be supported by systems to help manage QoS.

Voice over LTE (VoLTE) also comes with its own stringent requirements for minimal latency of voice packets, which may imply that even within services offered to the same user, voice may need to be given higher priority than pending data packets for the user. Normally, such complex conditions are met by implementation of scheduling algorithms that support guaranteed bit rate services such as the proportional fair scheduler (PFS), for example, but the implementation and testing of such solutions gets even more complicated with multiple users with differentiated priorities, classes, and services.

There are more solutions for implementing VoLTE support using existing IP multimedia subsystem (IMS) based core networks, which uses single radio voice call continuity (SRVCC) to address voice requirements. The IMS is used to control the handoff of the user to legacy networks that support voice. Thus, the operator needs to plan the solution with IMS support in mind when starting deployment.

Multivendor Interoperability

The original goals for LTE when the standardization efforts were made was to make standards in such a way that network elements from different vendors can interoperate seamlessly. Such a solution would give operators the benefit of being able to mix and match network elements as they desire to give them competitive advantage and prevent overdependence on any particular vendor implementation. This would have allowed operators to be able to negotiate price and services and also allows for the market to possibly gravitate toward the best performing network elements for appropriate functions.

Reality, as usual, is painting a different picture. It has been found that interoperability is not ensured between equipment from different vendors. In most cases, extensive testing is needed to conform that equipment and solutions are interoperable. Although the early entrant to the market has an advantage in terms of being the default implementation to which the later vendor needs to comply, the fact remains that true multivendor interoperability still remains a dream. Not only does in take too much effort and testing to ensure interoperability, but in some cases, it also implies that existing solutions provided by vendors need to be contractually maintainable and have support for further improvements or corrections for interoperability, which may not be the case for many implementations already deployed in the field.

All of this ends up adding to the overall cost for deployment and maintenance, especially in some cases when specific vendor solutions need to operate together due to network planning in some particular sites or locations. Tracking such issues and managing them closely are the only options available to the operator to ensure successful deployments and good user experiences when they move between different vendor network elements.

Issues Related to Backhaul

LTE as a technology has been designed to provide very high speeds on the radio UE side. If we trace back to earlier technologies like 2G or 3G traditionally, the radio, including UE and NodeB, has been the side that has limited networks' throughput. With the removal of that limitation, experts perceived that the attention would shift back to the backhaul for being able to support the required bandwidth. Operators not only need to be able to design the backhaul to be able to support required load generated by LTE terminals with very high data capabilities, but they also need to be able to add required additional capacity as needed by the growing network and subscriber needs.

Also, as an improvement in the architecture from 3G, LTE introduces the eNodeB as a single node that collects the functions of both the radio network controller (RNC) and the base station. In 3G networks, operators can plan a layered approach, with the RNCs aggregating the connections to the base stations and then being connected in a limited manner to the backhaul (core network). The LTE collapsing of the radio nodes into the eNodeB has also raised a related requirement of eNodeBs themselves being connected to one another, along with the need to be connected to the core network elements, thus leading to a mesh structure.

Hence, operators need to be very clear as to how they will achieve the required capacity in backhaul and yet be able to support such complex requirements for high capacity from LTE network deployments. This also means there needs to be sufficient investments made to realize and implement such a powerful backhaul capacity to handle the current and future LTE deployments.

Environment Issues

Aside from the issues discussed above, there are some challenges inherent to the technology and ecosystem that is evolving LTE development. This section addresses such issues, which are not only necessarily technology related, but also are inherent to the complexity of the technology and the environment under which such development is happening.

We discuss issues relating to UE, issues with the execution of complex projects where all network elements, including UE, eNodeB, and the EPC, are evolving at the same time. Also, we highlighted the role that is played to a certain extent by standardization efforts and limitations. Some of these issues are not necessarily unique to LTE; but they need to be understood and acknowledged by the operator, if only to get a better handle on managing the challenging task of deployment under such conditions.

UE Maturity

During the development of any new technology or feature, there is always a lack of valid UE that could be used during network element (NE) development to validate the functionality of the NE or feature with assurance (from the eNodeB point of view). Mostly, this is due to the fact that the UE is also being developed in parallel to the eNodeB development timeline. In such scenarios, the NE development proceeds with the usage of appropriate simulation tools to simulate UE behavior.

■ **Note**   What is valid for the eNodeB is also valid for the LTE UE development. Hence, UE developers too should be managing the lack of an eNodeB to validate the new feature.

In the absence of a real NE, development features get validated against simulated NEs, with simulated interfaces and multiple assumptions about the feature and technology (where the specifications are not precise or leave room for interpretation). Hence, there are bound to be integration issues when the commercial UEs do become available. In cases where cooperation agreements between network development and UE vendors exist, such issues possibly get addressed better in extended integration testing. In most cases though, this implies issues when multiple commercial UEs diverge in their implementation or interpretation of standards.

As a corollary to the above, where there are debug versions of UEs released, to help testing of other NEs, like eNodeBs, support may not be available for new features that are needed. Where there are commercial UEs available for testing, they may not provide enough debugging or logging capabilities to be of use during feature development and debugging.

Feature Availability

As discussed in the previous section, when all NEs are under development, planning integration testing and the rollout of a feature could be very difficult tasks.

It could be that the standardization plans for the feature are made available for some projected period, requiring the network and UE vendors to commit to some date based on the same, so operators, in turn, could plan appropriate times for integration and field testing and deployment of the feature and a subscriber can be informed about the usage of such a feature and how it could benefit them in achieving their personal or business goals.

Now, as always happens, Murphy's law could kick in, the best laid plans could go astray and delays could get introduced in all these processes. Essentially, the above process is like hitting a moving target and, depending on how much of a float is planned, the operator could absorb some of the delays. Being part of such a complex ecosystem inherently creates such dependency risks, and all stakeholders need to work closely to be able to minimize big changes in plans as much as possible and keep surprises to a minimum. Of course, safe project planning in terms of planning additional time as a buffer could help mitigate the issues to a certain extent.

Standardization Delays

Much of LTE development has been rigorously driven by extremely dedicated people working as part of the standardization committees under the aegis of the 3GPP.

It must be remembered though that standardization efforts are driven by people who work mostly for different participant companies that are trying to promote the agenda of their employer along with developing the standard. Hence, in spite of the best interests of the people involved, there may be issues with specifications for some standards and delays may be inevitable. It may also be that only when some standards are defined that further issues come up, which necessitates further specification efforts to be resolved. This is especially true for LTE where the standards are being developed for some problems that have not been solved at all until now, like SON, for example. Hence, SON will continue to be refined and be deployable only with LTE-Advanced, and such delays cannot be avoided. Operators must therefore be prudent and keep a wary eye on the standardization progress of important features in order to know well in advance if delays are imminent so that they can pursue alternate solutions wherever possible.

Patent Costs

If there is one moral that has been reemphasized through all the patent battles in recent times, it is that patents cost money and are really valuable. It is worth noting that companies pursue patents for many reasons. First, patents grant a company an advantage for an innovation that they have implemented and hence should provide avenues to monetize the same through licensing costs. Second, patents are useful to negotiate with a competitor who has a complementary set of patents to be able to cross-license the patents and make sure both are able to share advantages in a respectable manner. And third, patents are also used as a corporation weapon to destabilize competition by citing patent violations and ensuring that the competitor is unable to sells its product. This latter reason has been seen being actively played out in the past few years in courts all over the world between Samsung and Apple.

Coming back to LTE though, it was recognized very early on that allowing such patents to be granted will make life very difficult for many companies to offer product solutions, and the innovations will not be coming forth as a few companies with specific and crucial patents will stifle innovation, increase costs of the UEs and solutions to unmanageable levels, and in the long term prevent LTE from being adopted, developed, or deployed. So, to control such intellectual property rights (IPR) costs, a few like-minded companies with key patents in LTE, namely Ericsson, NSN, Nokia, NEC, and Nextwave wireless, collectively agreed to minimum royalty payments for their shared patent use in single digits of the handset sale price and to not exceed more than $10 for LTE modems in Netbooks (see http://www.ericsson.com/news/1209031).

It is also worthwhile to note that key players like Qualcomm are not part of this arrangement. Also, other big players in LTE like Huawei, Broadcom, and Texas Instruments are also not part of the above consortium. It is also clear that there are lots of innovation reports still being filed in all key and crucial areas of LTE, such as line interference management, SON, and handover optimizations, which implies that patent battles are far from over for LTE systems.

This should be of much concern to operators as the mobile devices they are planning to roll out may become embroiled in patent wars and may get banned from being sold. Deployments could get delayed, UEs could end up costing more, and consumers may, in the meantime, find other offerings to be more interesting. Also, vendors may have to find alternate ways to implement a feature or solution to a problem to avoid patent infringement, and the associated costs could end up delaying the release of a particular model or solution too.

MICROSOFT AND THE ANDROID PATENT MONEY TRAIN

To understand the cost of patents and the effect this can have on companies, we need go no further than Microsoft, whom some industry watchers project is making more money from Android devices than its own Windows phone division. Analysts estimate that Microsoft must be making nearly $2 billion every financial year, just from its Android licensing agreements (see http://www.zdnet.com/microsoft-is-making-2bn-a-year-on-android-licensing-five-times-more-than-windows-phone-7000022936/). So how exactly did Microsoft end up making so much money out of Android device sales?

Microsoft has been claiming violations on its patents by open source Linux software for quite a long time. In 2007, Microsoft made claims about Linux violating close to 235 software patents that were owned by Microsoft (http://archive.fortune.com/magazines/fortune/fortune_archive/2007/05/28/100033867/index.htm?source=yahoo_quote). In the previous year, Microsoft had already signed an interoperability pact with Novell, which though touted at that time to be a deal to promote SUSE Linux, was widely seen by analysts as protection offered by Microsoft to SUSE Linux users from patent violation damages (http://www.microsoft.com/en-us/news/press/2006/nov06/11-02msnovellpr.aspx). Novell had already been recognized as the owner of UNIX copyright in a case brought out by SCO against Linux vendors (http://www.groklaw.net/pdf2/Novell-846.pdf). So when Google started promoting the Android operating system as open source software, the fact that it is based on a Linux kernel made it vulnerable toward patent infringement suits. In 2011, Microsoft won a key patent decision that Motorola mobility violated Microsoft's patents in making its Android handsets (http://www.theguardian.com/technology/2011/dec/20/itc-microsoft-motorola-patent-android). Though the final decision has yet to be determined (http://www.microsoft.com/Investor/EarningsAndFinancials/Earnings/FinancialStatements/FY14/Q3/IRFinancialStatementsPopups.aspx?tag=us-gaap:CommitmentsAndContingenciesDisclosureTextBlock&title=Commitments%20and%20contingencies), the indications were clear that Google's acquisition of Motorola's patents did not prevent Android devices from being drawn into patent litigations suits by Microsoft. In the same year, multiple licensing deals between Microsoft and Android device makers, including big names like HTC, Samsung, and LG, were announced (http://www.networkworld.com/article/2180926/software/microsoft-inks-licensing-deals-with-two-more-android-makers.html).

In recent times, with the popularity of Android systems, many more Android device makers, including Amazon, have joined the list of companies who have entered into agreements with Microsoft. So, Microsoft's strategy to diversify its software patent portfolio is paying rich dividends to the tune of offsetting the losses it is facing from its own device businesses. More recently, Apple and Samsung are still embattled in further patent violation warfare, which could have more implications for Android device manufacturers in pushing up licensing costs (http://en.wikipedia.org/wiki/Apple_Inc._v._Samsung_Electronics_Co.,_Ltd..).

Business Challenges

In the previous section, we discussed issues related to LTE as a technology and how different aspects of the solution development could affect deployment and delay plans to roll out. This section will discuss issues related to business planning aspects of LTE deployments, which, though not numerous, are still very important in terms of impacts and in need of a thorough understanding and appreciation.

Investment Issues

As mentioned previously, LTE was designed from the ground up to provide the next futuristic network with very high data rates and strict targets to achieve QoS and latency issues. Also, there were strict performance criteria specified for various aspects of the solution as seen from the subscribers' perspective.

■ **Note**   These performance criteria are discussed in Chapter 1, with overall guideline requirements for LTE.

In order to meet these stringent requirements, newer NEs were introduced in the LTE network architecture, both in the radio network and on the core network side, when compared with 3G. Thus, we have NEs, including UEs that are new, that have much more complex functionality to accomplish. This directly implies a few things. Operators mostly are unable to reuse their current networks and need to invest in building their core and access networks with the newer NEs. Of course, some vendors are innovatively addressing such concerns by introducing newer 3G network elements that are LTE ready in the sense that they reduce the network deployment costs to just upgrades-for-LTE kind of solutions. Yet, predominantly, operators are required to invest upfront to make and deploy the LTE networks.

In times of financial turmoil, as existed in much of 2012 in international markets, this would mean that a majority of these decisions cannot be absorbed by operators because huge investments in such a financial climate may not be feasible. Also, unless operators are of such a size as to have surplus cash available to plan and make such deployments, they are going to be dependent on external funding to enable such deployments. Such borrowings, however, carry periods for interest calculations and need to be factored into the plans for deployment, and they further constrain the timelines by which operators can plan and execute their deployment and to be able to fulfill commercial obligations to the creditors in a timely manner. Coupled with the inherent challenges discussed in the previous section, this really is an arduous task.

Average Revenue per User and Return on Investment Periods

To make any business plan work, there needs to be elements of cost and modeling of expected revenue to be worked out so that subsequent periods of business can be simulated and some sort of profit projections can be made.

In the cellular world, the most common key performance indicator from revenues perspective is average revenue per user (ARPU). In simple terms, this could equate to the revenue generated by an operator divided by the number of users or subscribers supported by the operator. Hence, there is a way to find out how much one user is contributing to the margins of the operator and also determine business health through the service offering.

The return of investment (ROI) is the period over which a business needs to be operational to be able to start making enough money to tide over the investments made and hence start seeing profits. Businesses cannot expect to see any real profits until the ROI period is accomplished.

The key challenge with LTE network rollouts for the operator will be generating enough revenue from the services to the users to be able to have a high enough ARPU so that the ROI period is low enough to sustain interest of the investors and creditors. This is a pretty difficult task! For the proliferation of flat rate plans for a fixed capacity offering (in terms of gigabytes), you have to take away the ability of operators to specialize their offering as a premium service. It has long been the case that call rates for voice services are being pushed down due to competition and pressure from market regulators linked to the government. Even roaming offerings are no longer able to generate revenue as agencies are trying to minimize the impact on consumers as much as possible. So, operators are forced to innovate and differentiate their offerings and services enough so users are ready to pay a premium price or top dollar for their services. Also, as the focus moves more to the content that users can use, operators need to work with content providers so they don't lose any more relevance as meaningful players who can offer services and make real money in doing so.

The recent trends for major telecommunication providers indicate the following concerns in profitability as seen in operating the business landscape:

- Earnings indicators like EBITDA have been falling for the past two years.

- Returns on capital employed are also showing a downward trend.

- Voice revenues continue to fall even while mobile broadband picks up pace.

The Changing Marketplace

As discussed previously, the investments being made and the services being offered with some specific targets in mind can be made by the operator, keeping in mind certain assumptions about user behavior and applications that are targeted.

In the event that the market produces some stunning innovations, this could potentially challenge and turn the plans made by the operator upside down. For example, not many could have anticipated that the Android operating system would revolutionize the market for UEs in the way it has. Also, it brought a paradigm shift where users are ready to pay money for over the top (OTT) applications that are not necessarily basic services that work as a backbone. The longer a plan takes to roll out, the more chances that some disruptive innovation or application can change the market for better or for worse.

In such an environment, operators are advised to target routes to better profitability in the following ways:

- Provide differentiated service and pricing models

- Partner more with OTT application providers

- Improve network efficiency significantly

A Survey of LTE Deployments Around the World

Having seen the challenges that exist for LTE deployments, let's assess the ways network operators around the world have gone about their deployments. Central to this analysis is a categorization of deployment strategies into single radio access network (RAN) vs. network overlay.

In single RAN strategy, the network gets upgraded to support multimode, multistandard base stations that can help the operator deploy future proof technologies together. The following characteristics apply to the single RAN:

- Base stations deployed have multistandard capabilities, including 2G, 3G, along with LTE.

- In some cases the radio also has multimode support to work in TDD or FDD mode.

- There are reduced operational costs for managing the whole network.

- There are reduced site costs as converged nodes are deployed in the network.

- Overall upgrade of the networks may take time and also prove to be costly with the possibility of service disruption to existing subscribers.

For LTE network overlay strategy, the LTE networks are deployed and operated side by side with the existing 2G or 3G network, without doing an upgrade. The following characteristics apply to the LTE network overlay:

- New base stations are deployed for the LTE network.

- No immediate plans are made for upgrading 2G or 3G network base stations.

- There are reduced upgrade times and investment requirements.

- There is a need for separate systems to monitor existing 2G or 3G networks and new LTE networks.

- Possible upgrades are needed in the future depending on subscriber and services growth and the need for LTE expansion.

In deciding on a particular strategy, network operators will have to consider the constraints described in the previous sections in terms of spectrum availability, existing network investments and services, investment, and ROI roadmaps. As per the data available in a majority of cases, network operators have preferred the strategy of network overlay for their deployment. In the following sections, we discuss the overall strategy with specific highlights about some countries' LTE deployment.

South Korea

In South Korea we looked at how SK Telecom, KT, and LG U+ went about their LTE deployments.

SK Telecom adopted LTE network overlay as its strategy along with its existing 2G and 3G without going for an upgrade for the same. Its primary goal for the deployment was to meet the mobile broadband needs of its consumers. SK Telecom deployed its LTE services in 1.8Ghz with a bandwidth of 20Mhz. KT also adopted LTE network overlay to deploy LTE on the 800Mhz spectrum. It will also be able to utilize the 1.8Ghz spectrum it has after being allowed to discontinue the 2G services on the same. LG U+ went for a single RAN strategy using its existing CDMA infrastructure and deployed its LTE services using 2.1Ghz spectrum. It did not have a 3G service operational and hence the strategy was probably easier to implement.

Most Korean operators are looking to augment their LTE macro networks with small cell deployments to fill the gaps in residential areas and to continue to provide good coverage and services to its subscribers.

Japan

In Japan we looked at how NTT Docomo, KDDI, and SoftBank Mobile went about their LTE deployments.

NTT Docomo adopted the LTE network overlay strategy for its LTE services deployment in the 2.1Ghz spectrum. KDDI also adopted the LTE network overlay strategy for its LTE services in the 800Mhz spectrum band. KDDI is also planning to deploy in 1.5Ghz spectrum for services covering urban and suburban areas. SoftBank Mobile also adopted the LTE network overlay for deployment of LTE services in the 2.1Ghz spectrum in FDD mode to coexist along with its high-speed packet access-plus services in the 900Mhz spectrum. SoftBank Mobile also plans for LTE TDD deployment in the 2.5Ghz spectrum.

Australia

In Australia we looked at how Telstra and Optus went about their LTE deployments.

Telstra opted for LTE network overlay strategy to ensure LTE service deployment did not affect its existing 2G and 3G network operations. Telstra targeted its existing 3G subscribers for the LTE services by offering dual-mode LTE/HSPA+ dongles. Telstra deployed LTE on the 1.8Ghz spectrum and plans to selectively refarm the 900MHz too.

The network operator Optus also used a network overlay strategy to introduce LTE services in refarmed 1.8GHz 2G spectrum. Optus acquired WiMax operator Vivid wireless to be able to deploy TD-LTE network with 98MHz bandwidth in the 2.3GHz spectrum. For the TD-LTE deployment Optus mostly needs to use a single RAN strategy.

United States

In the United States, we looked at network operators Verizon, MetroPCS, AT&T, and Sprint Nextel for their LTE deployment strategies.

Verizon wireless used a network overlay strategy for deploying its LTE network, for a faster and less expensive deployment, along with its existing 2G and 3G services in the 2.1GHz spectrum. Verizon also plans for a 700MHz LTE deployment with 10MHz bandwidth. The operator continues to upgrade its subscribers to its LTE network with continuing growth and expansion plans.

MetroPCS also used a network overlay strategy to deploy LTE services on top of its existing 2G CDMA services, totally skipping 3G. MetroPCS also worked on upgrading existing CDMA subscribers to a less costly enhanced voice data optimized Rev-A network to enable faster speeds without needing a costly LTE handset upgrade for the same. In the meantime, *T*-Mobile USA was upgrading its 3G infrastructure to offer 21Mbp speeds with HSPA+ service. T-Mobile USA was also acquiring AWS spectrum to be able to deploy LTE with its own network overlay strategy. But it also acquired MetroPCS to consolidate and become a leading provider.

AT&T also deployed LTE in a network overlay strategy, along with its HSPA+ services using 700MHz spectrum and also AWS spectrum. Interestingly, AT&T also operated a wide network of Wi-Fi hotspots.

Sprint is the only U.S. operator that deployed LTE with a single RAN strategy to enable it to upgrade its existing 2G and 3G networks. Sprint plans to invest in this strategy to improve on coverage, capacity, and overall data speeds. Sprint plans to optimally use the 5MHz of paired FDD spectrum in 1900MHz and needs to make long-term plans for the investments needed and to secure financial planning with a buy in from SoftBank of Japan. Also Sprint strategically acquired Clearwire, with its 4G network having 160MHz bandwidth in the 2.5GHz spectrum, to deploy a TD-LTE network.

Traffic Profiles and Other Evolution Challenges

When the operators plan and deploy solutions, they make assumptions about the kind of traffic that different subscribers want, the services that subscribers will be using, the bit rates that will be desired, and the number of devices that will be accessing the network.

■ **Note** For a more rigorous treatment of these, refer to Chapter 1: parameters to be taken into account when dimensioning the network. Such parameters are also used for dimensioning the network to ensure QoS for all the service users and different applications.

However, it is easy to see that the telecom market dynamics keep changing all the time. We see changes in subscriber patterns, devices usage, and many other aspects. This section initially takes a look at some trends that can help us understand this dynamic nature, before we try to analyze the future trends to take into account.

Recent Trends in Telecom Customer Profiles Evolution
Usage of Dongles vs. Smartphones

Originally, subscribers who looked for connectivity to continue to have access to their work and hence needed mobile broadband access with their laptops purchased dongles instead of a smartphone, which was a device that helped one get e-mail and other important applications like messaging.

Now comes the interesting part. Depending on how the smartphone works in terms of idle time handling, smartphones could end up generating a lot of signaling traffic in comparison to dongles. One such study by NSN (albeit in 3G networks) found that even though dongles accounted for 60% of the data traffic load, they generated only 1% of the signaling load.

This is due to the fact that the dongles were getting connected and staying connected, whereas smartphones were aggressively optimizing power management and hence were becoming a new state called fast dormancy handling, where they were switching into RRC idle states very quickly.

Another key aspect of the dongle tends to be that most of them support only data connections vs. smartphones that have to support traditional customer service–based services of voice, text messages, and data connections. Hence, dongle implementations tend to be simpler as the complexity of connection management and other settings is managed by the connection management software in the laptop. This remains true even in cases of dongles that support voice. Hence, dongles cost a lot less than the equivalent smartphones.

By keeping track of a variety of devices getting connected in the network, the operator can continue to remain alert about trends of subscriber usage. For example, the following observations were made on Vodacom LTE networks in 2011 (`http://mybroadband.co.za/news/broadband/39919-data-usage-smartphones-vs-dongles.html`):

- The average data consumed by dongles grew only by 10% year over year, whereas data consumed by smartphones saw a 100% increase.

- The ratio of dongles to smartphones changed from roughly 80:20 to 65:35 by the end of the year.

- Vodacom had a total of 1.1 million dongles and 4.1 million active smartphone subscribers by the end of the year.

Smartphones are definitely going to continue to grow over dongles, but they will still be affected by price and data plans support provided by operators.

Further studies in consumer behavior and sentiment (`http://www.marketingmagazine.co.uk/article/1054529/research-charts-death-dongle-smartphone`) give credence to dongles being preferred by business savvy subscribers only. In this survey made in the United Kingdom in 2011, the number of respondents who preferred a dongle fell drastically from 20% in the previous year to 7%. At the same time, smartphone penetration keeps increasing, with 35% owning a smartphone in 2009, and doubled the same amount in the previous year. Also, 60% of the respondents indicate that they would be buying a smartphone.

Trends in Data vs. Voice Usage

Initial LTE networks were deployed with data-only plans and used existing 2G or 3G networks for voice support. Currently though, VoLTE has been specified and also implemented by many vendors as part of their solutions.

It is interesting to note that with additional smartphones getting introduced into the market, the usage of traditional voice keeps coming down in comparison to data usage in same periods. One study of Finnish iPhone users shows data over a 10-month period in 2011-2012 (`http://www.forbes.com/sites/terokuittinen/2012/10/15/as-iphone-mobile-data-usage-soars-voice-calls-dive/`), where data usage has seen a spike of over 68% per subscriber, as shown in Figure 3-1.

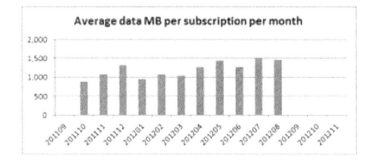

Figure 3-1. *Average date per month*

Also, in the same period the average voice minutes per subscriber dropped by over 13%. It was observed that traditional text messaging too declined by the same percentage (Figure 3-2).

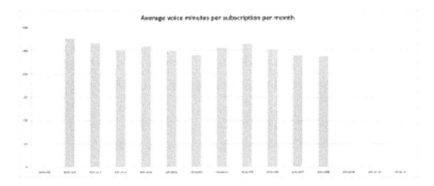

Figure 3-2. *Average voice minutes*

It has to be noted that this study is based on iPhone usage patterns alone. Also, the trend of similar data usage is being observed across high-end smartphones in Finland, the United States, and the United Kingdom, independent of network operators and across different networks. It does appear that newer smartphones, which allow higher data rates to be enabled, coupled with newer OTT applications make subscriber data usage trends more uniform.

Elsewhere, as illustrated in another study, the trend is that data are becoming the premium service along with decreasing voice spend (http://www.worldwideworx.com/mobile-data/). Average user cell phone spending has increased from 8% to 12% over an 18-month period. And voice spend during the same period went down from 77% to 73%.

The demography of mobile subscribers also plays a crucial role in a trend of decline in voice usage. This is shown by a recent survey of mobile data usage by teens in the United States (http://www.nielsen.com/us/en/newswire/2011/new-mobile-obsession-u-s-teens-triple-data-usage.html). Average mobile data usage has increased by 256% for teens and shows a definite increase across all age groups in general, as shown in Figure 3-3.

Figure 3-3. *Monthly data usage by age*

Not surprisingly, voice usage went down for the same group by 17%, from an average of 685 minutes to 572 minutes. Most of the respondents attributed this to messaging being "faster, easier and being more fun."

Growth of Internet and Smartphone Usage Across the World

As a running theme in the telecom landscape, consumer growth patterns and traffic growth continue to be driven strongly by access to the Internet. Mobile broadband services and access of the same through smartphones continue to be critical profitability factors for operators.

The proportion of Internet users across the world gives us a good idea about where the penetration is already at a high level. Markets that have high Internet penetration tend to be more mature in their use of the Internet. Also, they have a higher demand for advanced value-added services in comparison to more developing areas, where primary access to the Internet is still developing. The statistics presented in Figure 3-4 from Internet World Stats provide a good picture of the proportion of Internet users across the world by the end of 2013.

Internet Users in the World
Distribution by World Regions - 2013 Q4

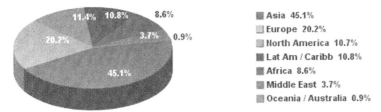

11.4% 10.8% 8.6%
20.2% 3.7% 0.9%
45.1%

- Asia 45.1%
- Europe 20.2%
- North America 10.7%
- Lat Am / Caribb 10.8%
- Africa 8.6%
- Middle East 3.7%
- Oceania / Australia 0.9%

Source: Internet World Stats - www.internetworldstats.com/stats.htm
Basis: 2,802,478,934 Internet users on Dec 31, 2013
Copyright © 2014, Miniwatts Marketing Group

Figure 3-4. *Internet use by the end of 2013*

It is clear from Figure 3-4 that bigger demographies have a larger presence in the Internet. Asia dominates as a highly populated region and hence it is more interesting to see the proportion of population that has access to the Internet. As illustrated in Figure 3-5, from the same period we see a worldwide total penetration of Internet at only 39%.

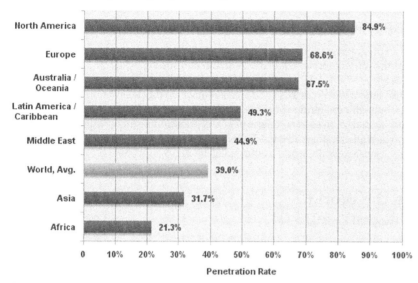

**World Internet Penetration Rates
by Geographic Regions - 2013 Q4**

Source: Internet World Stats - www.internetworldststs.com/stats.htm
Penetration Rates are based on a world population of 7,181,858,619
and 2,802,478,934 estimated Internet users on December 31, 2013.
Copyright © 2014, Miniwatts Marketing Group

Figure 3-5. *Worldwide penetration of the Internet*

Also, the top 20 countries that use the Internet contribute to 70% of the total users, and further Internet penetration among the population gives us an indication of the maturity of the market in that country and the potential for differentiated services (`http://www.internetworldstats.com/top20.htm`). From the same data, it is very clear that some countries like India and China have had phenomenal growth rates from 2000 to 2013; yet their penetration rates are still low, indicating much scope for further growth potential.

Going further, as per Figure 3-6 from the IDC, as of 2012, 53% of smartphone consumers over the world access the Internet through their smartphones. Combining the Internet penetration with the smartphone access gives a very good indicator of the potential for smartphone-based mobile broadband access across different countries. This should be a critical part of operator assessments for business potential in that region.

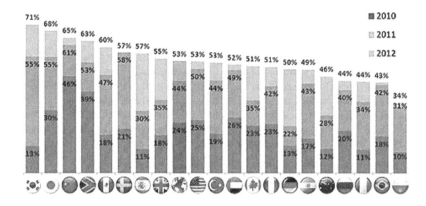

Figure 3-6. *Percentage of smartphone owners using Internet on phone daily*

Furthermore, figures from Google Analytics for overall mobile traffic access numbers as a percentage of overall web traffic numbers give very encouraging inputs for operators:

- Total mobile traffic was up 139% on average from Q4 2011 to Q4 2012.

- Eighteen percent of total web traffic was coming from mobile devices by Q4 2012.

- Mobile traffic as a percentage of total website traffic nearly doubled from 10% to 18% from Q4 2011 to Q4 2012.

In fact, as per the projections from Morgan Stanley, mobile Internet users are poised to overtake desktop Internet users as of end of 2014, as shown in Figure 3-7.

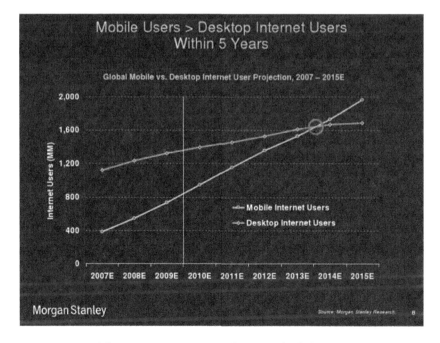

Figure 3-7. *Mobile Internet users are poised to overtake desktop Internet user*

More interestingly, the growth rates of early desktop Internet access in the 1990s (as measured with AOL and Netscape adoption) in comparison with mobile usage growth in the 2000s (as measured primarily by following Apple devices: iPhone/iTouch) leads to the following observations.

Adoption of Apple devices is almost 11 times faster than AOL and several times faster than Netscape. The 3G services act as an inflection point in helping enable access to more than 20% of cellular users to help accelerate mobile Internet access. This proves to be inspirational for LTE operators as LTE services could serve to take mobile Internet usage acceleration to the next level. This is especially true with the increasing popularity of services that demand higher bandwidths, like video, which NSN forecasts will account for 60% of all mobile traffic in 2013.

The IDC Predications 2014 (`http://www.idc.com/research/Predictions14/index.jsp`) further cement some of the observations made in the earlier sections:

- Smartphone and tablet sales are outgunning PC sales by nearly 2.5 times or 250%.

- Apple continues to see strong iPhone and iPad sales to retain a value advantage of nearly double its competition, but it still is outnumbered by Android devices with a volume of one-third or a ratio of 1:3.

- Google Play Store catches up with the App Store to narrow down revenue differences.

- Cloud spending is expected to surge to nearly $100 billion, for a growth rate of 25%.

- Data volumes are expected to reach 6 trillion terabytes, pushing the spending on big data analytics by 30%.

- The Internet of Things (IoT) remains very promising, with 30 billion endpoints and $8.9 trillion in revenue expected by 2020.

The ITU-T ICT facts and figures for 2014 (`http://www.itu.int/en/ITU-D/Statistics/Pages/facts/default.aspx`) add some very interesting insights into some of the items we have been discussing in the preceding section. Some of these include:

- There are 2.3 billion mobile broadband subscriptions, with developing countries contributing up to 55%.

- Mobile broadband is growing at double the rate in developing countries as compared to developed countries.

- Mobile broadband penetration rate is expected to reach a global value of 32% by the end of 2014, with developing countries still only being 21% covered vs. 84% in developed countries.

- The penetration rate is almost double that of 2011.

- Africa leads in mobile broadband growth from 2% in 2010 and to 20% in 2014.

- Mobile subscriptions will reach almost 7 billion by the end of 2014, with a penetration rate of 96%, with more than half of these coming from Asia-Pacific region.

- Mobile cellular growth rates are at the lowest global level of 2.6%, which indicates saturation in the markets globally, with developing countries still expanding twice as much as developed countries.

- Fixed broadband growth is slowing down in developing countries.

- By the end of 2014, nearly 3 billion people (40% of world population) will be using the Internet, with 66% of the same hailing from developing countries.

- While 44% of world households will have an Internet connection, only 10% of households in Africa enjoy this technology.

- The percentage of fixed broadband users who enjoy more than 10Mbit/s speeds still remains lower in developing countries when compared to developed countries.

All of the above indicators imply that there is still good potential for enabling high-speed mobile broadband access and applications that exploit the same.

■ **Note**   For more detailed analysis of traffic profiles and dimensioning inputs, see Chapter 1.

Future Traffic Profiles and Trends

Having seen how the Internet and mobile Internet devices are all shaping up, it is interesting to see what sort of trends are seen in the near horizon of five to seven years and what changes will be happening in that same timeframe. It is very important for operators to understand that all of these trends represent real opportunities for growth and profitability and hence need to be factored in when planning for 4G network, and beyond, deployment.

In the following sections, we list the major trends as forecasted from the following listed reports:

- Vision 2020 whitepaper final from NSN (http://networks.nokia.com/file/26156/technology-vision-2020-white-paper)

- Traffic and Market report June 2012 from Ericsson (http://www.ericsson.com/res/docs/2012/traffic_and_market_report_june_2012.pdf)

- IDC predictions 2013—competing on the 3rd platform (http://www.idc.com/research/Predictions13/downloadable/238044.pdf)

- Internet Trends by Mary Meeker, Morgan Stanley April 12, 2010 (http://www.slideshare.net/malaparte/morgan-stanley-internet-trends-mary-meeker-20100412)

- Cisco Visual Networking Index: Forecast and Methodology, 2012–2017 (http://www.slideshare.net/andrewwilliamsjr/cisco-visual-networking-index-forecasting-and-methodology-2012-2017)

- McKinsey—MGI_Disruptive_technologies_Executive_summary_May2013 (http://www.mckinsey.com/~/media/McKinsey/dotcom/Insights%20and%20pubs/MGI/Research/Technology%20and%20Innovation/Disruptive%20technologies/MGI_Disruptive_technologies_Executive_summary_May2013.ashx)

- MGI_IT_enabled_trends_Report_May 2013_v2 (http://www.mckinsey.com/insights/high_tech_telecoms_internet/~/media/mckinsey/dotcom/insights/high%20tech%20telecoms%20internet/ten%20it-enabled%20business%20trends%20for%20the%20decade%20ahead/mgi_it_enabled_trends_report_may%202013_v2.ashx)

One thing that is also very clear is that in the following sections, we are trying to do some crystal ball gazing to really delve into what the future holds in terms of areas of interest and impact to the telecom operators, especially given that 4G deployments are going to have much more momentum. While crystal ball gazing is good for getting a future outlook, one should also be clear upfront that our projections may not come true or may come true only to a partial extent. Also, it is important to note that in the telecom industry, as in other sectors, it is not easy to estimate the impact of certain technologies from the buzz existing about the same technology in Internet, social blogging, and other technology-related news sites. Clearly, mobile Internet is generating enough revenue currently and has impacted many businesses already by enabling online customers through mobile devices. Other key technologies have enough potential and impact for the 4G operator to consider, such as mobile Internet, Cloud technology, the IoT, and automation of knowledge work.

The Internet of Things

The term Internet of Things was originally coined by Kavin Ashton as part of a presentation to Procter and Gamble (`http://www.rfidjournal.com/articles/view?4986`). What started originally as a method of managing things and devices with radio-frequency identification (RFID) enablement has now grown to cover a multitude of things as more and more analysts have joined the bandwagon. As of now, the Internet of Things is meant to include everyday objects that have the following properties: objects can be read, located, addressed, and controlled via the Internet.

The technologies used for accessing the Internet could be through RFID, WLAN, wired networks, and any other methods, which could encompass things like ultra light SIMs for other radio access technologies like 3G or LTE, which could be embedded into the devices.

Some recent research from McKinsey even projects the Internet of Things to have morphed into what they call the *Internet of All Things*, emphasizing the nature of the trend itself, to encompass all things that come onto the Internet, including items that we would normally not associate with the Internet, like clothing, food, and even shelter. The paper defines the Internet of All things, as follows:

> *Linking machinery, equipment, and other physical assets with networked sensors and actuators to capture data and manage performance, enabling machines to collaborate and even act on new information independently.*

The following application areas are seen as having major potential for the IoT:

- Remote monitoring of assets, systems, and people

- Performing preventive maintenance and improving systems management with data collected in real time

- Autonomous optimization of systems with complex closed-loop decision making

- Health applications where people can get a quantified assessment of their overall health, well-being, and monitoring

Additional areas that are still being explored for more impact in applications include:

- Sensor networks made up of distributed sensors, which are still evolving, some as small as smart dust that could help collect more information about buildings, vehicles, and other places that need to have Internet access and applications to use the same

- Ubiquitous positioning applications to locate and use objects residing indoors or outdoors or even underground, where reach through normal signaling may be inadequate

- Biometrics applications, where systems and things could identify people using their biometric footprint like fingerprints, facial scans, iris scans, etc.

- Machine vision using objects enabled with cameras that could interwork with applications like Augmented Vision, to give more context-based information. For example, Google Glasses is one such application.

Where all these applications lie in relation to IoT evolution is more evident in the roadmap shown in Figure 3-8. As per the current state of practice, we have barely scratched the surface of IoT applications, and a lot more improvements and capabilities are planned for the coming decades.

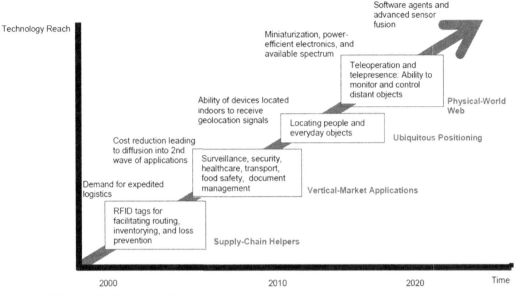

TECHNOLOGY ROADMAP: THE INTERNET OF THINGS

Source: SRI Consulting Business Intelligence

Figure 3-8. *Roadmap of the future of the Internet of Things*

As can be seen in Figure 3-8, Supply Chain management and inventory applications have already started using IoT to manage their products using RFID-based solutions. What is interesting in this roadmap is that positioning applications are about to get more traction toward the middle of this decade. But the real growth of IoT will come when teleoperation and the telepresence of objects become enabled as it would mean decisions on the following:

- How the objects would access the Internet:
  - Would they directly access the Internet or would they talk to a local information collector that would bridge the Internet?
- What would be the power consumption of the objects?
- What would be the form factor of such objects?
- What kind of data would need to be transmitted and received?
- How often would such data transmission need to happen?
- Would the objects communicate directly to other objects or people also?
  - What would be the protocol followed in such communications?
  - Would there be only data communicated or some form of voice communication also posited?
- What would be the number of such objects on the network?
- What is the cost of failure to the objects and to the applications?

We will address these questions later in this section in the context of their impact on 4G for such Internet of Things. Also, we will define the traffic profile for the IoT in that same discussion. The following section will focus more on the top impediments to the IoT as of now so you get an idea as to the state of practice of the IoT.

Top Challenges for Internet of Things

Standardization

Standardization has been identified as one of the key challenges facing a larger adoption of the IoT by a ITU-T report on this in 2007, and it is still one the major concerns in further development of the IoT. Even a recent consortium on the IoT held in 2013 observed that standardization in Cloud access technologies could be the major impairment for the IoT.

In this regard, a 2012 report, from the European Research Cluster on IoT, identified the following aspects for architecture development:

- Structure reference frameworks for logical hardware and software components still need to be developed and refined.

- Questions of object identification, virtualization, and decentralization still need to be finalized.

- The interoperability of the IoT across application sectors needs to be ensured.

Security and Privacy

As with everything else related to the Internet, issues about security and privacy dominate the IoT. With the number of devices that will be getting on to the Internet directly or indirectly, there are key questions about security aspects that need to be addressed.

Risks remain about vulnerabilities related to security issues that could lead to annoyances and also losses of an economic nature to the businesses involved. Also, one can only imagine what havoc can be wrecked by those who could take control of such devices via the Internet and could harm or impair many systems by creating problems that range from household issues to complex industrial shutdowns.

As with sensitive information collected by social networks today, questions remain about privacy concerns for the huge amount of data that would be gathered, collected, analyzed, and disseminated to a wide variety of manual and automated systems. With the prospect that additional devices could in turn be using the data collected in other ways, the complexity of the problems and rules that govern gain more importance. Also, different countries and businesses could have different laws regarding privacy of data, which also may need to be aligned and adhered to in making the IoT applications work together safely. Lifecycle processes that cover the data also need to be defined and adhered to.

Interoperability Testing

Standardization efforts are further needed to ensure that all the systems participating in the IoT remain compatible to one another. Interoperability testing is seen to be pretty challenging in such environments. By the nature of the IoT, objects and systems are meant to identify one another and operate together in increasingly manifold ways, placing a larger burden on testing efforts. Large-scale testing and pilots to confirm interoperability and further improvements to standards are expected to be crucial and essential in making things simpler.

Environmental Concerns

There are jokes doing the rounds that the latest touch-based smartphones with the biggest screens around are not so smart after all, as sometimes they run out of battery and hence remain "dumber than normal phones." Energy requirements and management would play key roles in future electronic devices. With the number of devices that may end up online on the Internet and power consumption requirements for these, there are valid questions that need to be answered about how energy impacts due to the IoT will be managed.

Also, electronics have a way of becoming outdated very easily. The industry itself seems to be fueling this rapid replacement of current models with newer ones, leading to *tons* of e-waste being generated around the cities of the modern world. It is expected that for whatever reasons (faulty devices, lower lifespan, becoming outdated), the IoT could end up adding to the e-waste generation and would hence need to be managed more actively and responsibly with the help of businesses and governments.

4G and the Internet of Things
The Case for LTE-Advanced and IoT

McKinsey estimates that there has been over a 300% increase in machine-to-machine device connections over the past five years. Clearly, there is an increasing trend of objects getting on to the Internet and interconnecting with other devices on the Internet. LTE as the leading 4G technology is primed to enable the IoT in the following ways:

- Nearly a trillion things could be connected to the Internet and more than 100 million machine-to-machine connections could be present. LTE networks are able to address so many devices due to close interworking with IPv6 for standardization.

- Billions of connected subscribers could be generating as much as 1GB data every day, and LTE networks are primed to be able to carry such high data volumes.

- LTE networks, with their very low latency targets, should be able to meet with real-time data delivery requirements of the IoT applications.

LTE and Small Devices

It is expected that objects and devices that want to get on to the Internet would need cost-effective solutions that would enable rapid adoption and deployment of LTE-based devices. NSN believes that LTE has great potential to enable all objects and networked things to come on to the Internet and manage the data explosion that would ensue.

Earlier we asked the question about how the objects would access the Internet. For the sake of our discussions here, we'll restrict ourselves to the following model for devices and objects to come on to the IoT, as it is more complex and more interesting.

- The objects or devices shall have embedded communication capability to implement one or more of the wireless access technologies, namely the LTE access technology.

- Customer applications that work on the IoT that are to be implemented on devices that control the data and format in which it must be sent to the Internet.

These models would imply that there are a lot of innovations waiting to happen in such a market where there is a huge demand for simplified "system on chips," which could be used to design and add IoT capability to any normal device or equipment discussed above. For example, SEQUANS communications has a brand of product lines based on Streamlite LTE (http://www.sequans.com/products-solutions/streamlitelte/). As seen in the following quote, the product is designed to be used with lots of daily devices:

> *Firefly is designed for connection to CE and M2M devices such as digital cameras, e-readers, security cameras, vending machines, digital signage, power meters, and health monitoring devices. It is also perfectly suited for integration into surface-mountable modules.*

Some of the technologies that have been discussed in this chapter are concerned with power consumption, and having a small footprint for the device can be seen in some excerpted product highlights such as:

- Throughput up to 50Mbps DL/25 Mbps UL

- 40 nm CMOS technology

- 4G-EZ ultra-low power technology

- High-performance LTE RFIC supplied by Fujitsu Semiconductor

- Dual RF ports

The Fujitsu MB86L13A, which the Firefly solution uses, is itself marketed as an IoT ready LTE-optimized transceiver, and though it is primarily targeted for LTE mobile handsets, the vendor does claim support for additional devices. These devices, with the key use being a mobile Internet device, include dual RF ports, mobile phones, data cards, and embedded modules.

It is to be noted here as elsewhere that LTE as a standard has evolved to better cater to trends like the IoT for better interworking and optimization, much of which is part of LTE-Advanced specifications (Rel 10 and above), which is beyond the focus of this book. Also, it can be expected that there will be plenty of innovation in integration of IoT with LTE networks.

The following section gives some pointers to aspects of the LTE RAN, which could be tuned in anticipation of devices that participate in IoT:

- Data usage and frequency: IoT devices that connect to the Internet directly could work on the following two modes:

  - The devices could be more like sensors that need to send small chunks of data in real time in periodic intervals:

    - Traffic profiles: In such scenarios, the traffic and the bearers in uplink alone could be modeled after VoLTE bearers that also have similar characteristics.

    - Data dimensioning needs to be done for the size of the packets and the rates of the bearers assigned to ensure QoS is satisfied.

    - Latency requirements need to be checked from the point of view of the application, and this may also determine if retransmissions make sense. Would the application still be interested in a real-time data point that was missed?

  - The devices could be collecting data over a longer time to search for trend analysis and may come online periodically to send bigger chunks of data. Also, this could happen based on a trigger or message received by the device:

    - Traffic profiles: In such scenarios the traffic and the bearers in uplink alone could be modeled after non–real-time bearers, which could be default bearers.

    - Retransmissions would make sense here and bigger-sized packets could be used to ensure that the payload goes through.

    - The latency requirements may not be too strict here as more importance is placed on the data's correctness and validity.

    - All the above would need to be validated with the actual IoT application requirements.

Cloud Computing and Mobile Internet

We briefly discussed the IoT and the implications the technology and application of this hold for us in the future. To complete the discussion, we briefly review a couple of related technologies in Cloud computing and mobile Internet that enables the IoT and a host of other applications that are deemed to have a disruptive influence for the future in terms of potential business impact.

We have already discussed the growing trend of mobile Internet and how projections indicate that the same will quickly outgrow desktop access to become the dominant way in which the Internet will be accessed. Also, we have hinted that standardization of Cloud access technologies could enable faster deployment of the IoT and help in adoption of this idea.

As per the McKinsey report on disruptive technologies in 2013, the following are the projections for impacts on mobile Internet by 2025:

- By 2013, there has been an increase of six times in the sale of mobile devices since 2007.

- In 2013, 4.3 billion people remain unconnected, with a possible 1 billion workers that could use online transactions.

- By 2025, it is estimated the potential impact of mobile Internet will range from a low of $3.7 trillion to $10.8 trillion.

To get a sense of the impact of Cloud computing, we could peruse the following estimates:

- In an era ruled by Moore's law, it takes about 18 months to double server performance, but the Cloud now enables rentals to be so low as to make the cost of owning a server three times that of renting one in the Cloud.

- 2.7 billion people could be served from the Cloud using 50 million servers.

- There could be up to $3 trillion of IT spent that could potentially be on the Cloud.

- By 2025, it is estimated that the potential impact of Cloud computing will range from a low of $1.7 trillion to a high of $6.2 trillion.

So, how should all of this be of interest to mobile operators?

- As a mobile network service provider, you should look to capitalize on the Cloud and solidify your strategy.

- You must look to enable services through the Cloud and the applications that will enable the end users to take advantage of them. This could also include the ability to enable access to popular Cloud services through your mobile Internet.

- You could also design plans and services to make it easier for end users to use the Cloud for their data and services.

As a business that provides solutions to be deployed, your network roadmaps must reflect services that enable the Cloud as an integral part of the solution. You must brainstorm to understand which parts of the network can enable Cloud interactions directly and which parts could aggregate and interoperate with existing Cloud services.

Summary

This chapter started by looking at key challenges facing LTE deployment—those associated with the technology itself and also the business challenges that are related to making the investments necessary—and the uncertainty surrounding the market evolution.

From there we went through some concepts related to recent evolutions and trends in mobile and Internet usage, in terms of the different types of devices being used to access the Internet, and how mobile Internet growth is projected to overtake PC or laptop-based Internet access within the next few years.

We went through basic traffic profiling concepts and related dimensioning tools that would be needed by the operator to provision and plan for a deployment and how the subscriber's access and applications can impact the traffic profiles.

Next, we spent some time discussing the forecasts shared by major telecom players and analysts to understand what sort of future trends could be interesting for the operators. We examined one such technology, which is the Internet of Things. Also, we looked at some pointers on what aspects of LTE networks may need to be tuned to cater to the IoT as we understand it.

What you should be able to see through this chapter is that both LTE networks and the trends are evolving, and the projected trends should be closely followed so operators and vendors can take advantage of the potential economic value associated with these technologies.

CHAPTER 4

∎ ∎ ∎

Network Roadmaps

"Would you tell me, please, which way I ought to go from here?"

"That depends a good deal on where you want to get to," said the Cat.

"I don't much care where—" said Alice.

"Then it doesn't matter which way you go," said the Cat.

"—so long as I get SOMEWHERE," Alice added as an explanation.

"Oh, you're sure to do that," said the Cat, "if you only walk long enough."

Alice in Wonderland —Lewis Carroll

Let's face it—the network's business is a very tough business. There are too many stakeholders—operators, vendors, standardization, end users, technology, equipment, government, partners for production, delivery, and so on. Over and above this, we have already discussed the challenges facing the business climate—in terms of investment, projections, customer demand, usage profiles, traffic patterns and their evolution, and so forth. In such a complex business environment, how do operators ensure that their plans remain valid, relevant, and that they can stay competitive?

We strongly believe that road mapping as a process offers a structured approach to deal with multiple stakeholders and evolve a united vision to go toward the future. The roadmap serves to both maintain the course toward achieving certain business objectives for the present while also working in a direction for the collective future where the business and ecosystem can continue to flourish successfully and remain relevant.

This chapter starts by detailing the needs for a technology roadmap. We also look at what the levels of detail of such a roadmap could be and what timelines such roadmaps could target. From there, we evolve toward network roadmaps, and what they imply to the operator in terms of configuration options and models that could be used to support them.

We would like to set up the fundamentals of need for the roadmaps in this chapter so we can elaborate more in later chapters on how roadmaps can allow networks to evolve. Later, we'd like to offer a process to create and evolve a roadmap. We hope to drive home some important points though; to be able to appreciate the power of roadmaps one must first understand the need for a roadmap. Thereafter, one must understand enough detail, not only to be able to create a roadmap, but also to appreciate that the process of creating the roadmap is almost as important as the resultant roadmap itself.

What Is a Technology Roadmap?

A technology roadmap is the result of a strategic technology planning process that cooperatively identifies (1) a particular Industry's common product and process performance targets, (2) the technology alternatives and milestones for meeting these targets, and (3) a common technology path for research and development activities.

Introduction to Technology Road mapping: The Semiconductor Industry Association's Technology Road mapping Process SAND97-0666, April 1997

Any industry that gets established and flourishes does so based on some fundamental principles:

- There should be a strong consumer-driven need for the products that are produced by the industry.

- The industry must develop standards that help evolve an ecosystem of interworking products based on components.

- Multiple vendors are able to make products that work with one another, giving the consumer the ability to interchange parts of various solutions.

- The industry must be able to innovate constantly to match consumer expectations and drive further demand by generating future features that create revenue making.

In the telecom industry, the technology roadmap published by the consortium 3GPP keeps media interested and excited about top-line capabilities of future features planned in a technology like LTE-Advanced. At the same time, the nitty-gritty of implementing the roadmaps through standards helps companies innovate and cooperate to interwork and get the technology to be part of actual products. The roadmaps help lay a pathway for features that eventually get implemented and also give a structure for the companies to work with one another to evolve the items that get implemented.

Understand Need for a Roadmap

Do we really need a roadmap for all technologies? What are the specific characteristics that help identify or confirm the need for a roadmap? Toward answering these questions, let's briefly revisit some basics of technology definition.

tech·nol·o·gy

Noun

The application of scientific knowledge for practical purposes, esp. in industry: "computer technology"; "recycling technologies".

Machinery and equipment developed from such scientific knowledge.

Merriam-Webster's Dictionary

Note some key characteristics of this:

- Technology is oriented toward an application.

- The underlying knowledge on which the technology works is specific to the particular industry.

- There is an underlying scientific basis to the knowledge that makes up the technology.

Because technology is developed on the basis of very specific knowledge, there is a strong need to properly manage the technology itself. Technology management, and the process that is used, is almost as important as the technology itself. As any technology evolves, it tends to comprise both implicit and explicit knowledge. It is easier to capture explicit knowledge in terms of documents that accompany manifestation of a technology like a manual for a mobile phone. Implicit or tacit knowledge is better translated through experience sharing and other such trainings. Such knowledge definitely needs to be managed under the gambit of technology management.

> *Technology management addresses the effective identification, selection, acquisition, development, exploitation and protection of technologies (product, process and infrastructural) needed to maintain [and grow] a market position and business performance in accordance with the company's objectives.*

European Institute of Technology Management

Though the above definition explains technology management from the perspective of a company, we should understand that this very well applies to an industry too. It is important to retain focus on some valid points from this definition that we'll revisit later:

- A company's or industry's objectives demand specific market positions to be met or grown into so business performance satisfies the same.

- A company or industry needs to manage technological aspects with commercial impacts to ensure relevance to what is getting developed.

- There needs to be ways to identify, select, acquire, develop, exploit, and protect technologies that would help satisfy these needs.

Elements of the list above imply that companies need a way to ascertain or project needs over a time period in forms of commercial goals, which would then need to be met with specific technologies that are managed. Companies mostly organize work across several technical and financial departments to arrive at such a consensual document that captures the relevant information in terms of the growth the company expects to achieve, the financial measurements of these, and the technologies that help the company achieve the projected goals. A document that captures such information typically tends to have elements of a roadmap in the sense that:

- The final goals for the period are broken down into smaller goals, which are quantified and measurable.

- The smaller goals, limited by timelines, also have specific technological achievements to be made and validated.

- The milestones of such technological achievements tend to indicate features or subfeatures that need to be developed and incorporated as whole or part of a product that the company develops.

Functions of companies such as strategy development and forecasting typically develop positions about what the company needs to achieve in the future and helps formulate the dialog that needs to happen with the technical functions to arrive at what the company's projected path looks like. Any document that captures the end result becomes a roadmap that could be shared with the whole of the company to confirm and implement the collective vision that is intended to be achieved.

Formulation of a Technology Roadmap

Let's look at a fictional product meeting where key personnel from different parts of a product company are meeting to compare their notes and determine what should be happening with the product. The following is an example of a typical product meeting:

> *Actors*: Bob from Product Marketing, Alan from Engineering, David from Sales, and Rick from customer support.
>
> *Bob*: As I was saying, customers would like to know what features our product would be supporting in the subsequent releases. I have a long list of features that different customers want. So tell me, what can we do over this year and the coming year to make this happen?
>
> *Alan*: Engineering is pretty far behind the current commitments as it is and we surely would need to drop some features even to get current releases out. The question is which features do I drop?
>
> *David*: Team—I really need to give some clear directions to sales. We keep meeting lots of customers and I am not really sure if we are speaking about the correct features that we are focusing on. I would like to read from the same sheet so we get customers to look at the critical few features that we will be building in the coming few releases.
>
> *Rick*: Please remember that our customers see so many issues in the field currently, they are desperate to understand when and how we will be fixing these issues. With all the focus that we would be giving to the future, let's not forget our current woes, which we need to rectify to improve customer satisfaction.

So we can understand that different stakeholders have different needs for information about the product under development. In an ideal product development environment, all these concerns get addressed with the technology roadmap of the product. The ways in which the product gets developed depends on the particular road-mapping process the product company actually may follow.

▪ **Note**   We will be covering the possible processes for technology road mapping in more detail in Chapter 6.

In short though, the way in which the roadmap gets developed may depend on some of the following aspects:

- *Size of the organization*. Smaller companies may prefer shorter and more informal processes for roadmap development.

- *The number of stakeholders involved*. For organizations like 3GPP, where there are many stakeholders actively participating in the road-mapping process, this means a very formal process governed by workshops to collect input, followed by detailed plans for incorporation of common elements into the roadmap for a standard, such as the materials and documentation recorded about a 3GPP Rel 12 RAN workshop (http://www.3gpp.org/news-events/3gpp-news/1266-Future-Radio-in-3GPP).

- *Time and effort the organization is prepared to invest in the process.*

- *Position of the organization in the industry*. Companies in leadership positions may like to publish their roadmaps in all channels and help shape the future and get their followers to align to the same.

Also the form in which the roadmaps could be expressed also varies a lot, depending on existing organizational practices and some of the factors mentioned above, such as:

- Some roadmaps could be captured as simple textual statements describing the intent of the company to develop features in particular areas.

- Roadmaps could also be expressed in a graphical format with timelines expressed on an x axis and features and impacts being shown on a y axis. Figure 4-1, the roadmap depicting the Internet of Things, is an example of a graphical roadmap.

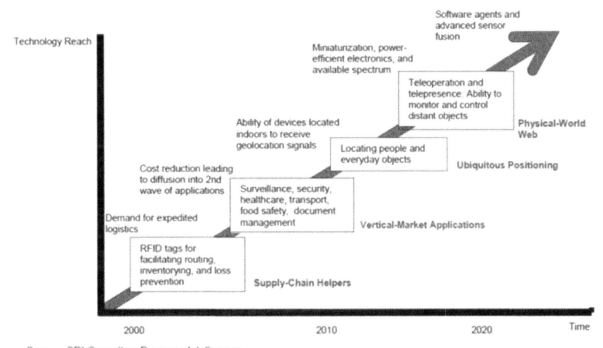

Figure 4-1. *Internet of Things roadmap*

- Most commonly though, roadmaps tend to get developed and communicated through a set of slides or documents giving a detailed list of features like the different versions of the product, as well as showing the timelines and a graphical representation of the targets for the features through their impact.

In spite of the differences in the ways roadmaps may get developed, represented, and communicated, most roadmaps should adhere to some standard maxims or implicit requirements about them. The most important requirement for any roadmap is that it should be able to address the different needs of different stakeholders to get sufficient information in sufficient detail. What we mean here is that for those stakeholders who are very interested to understand the features of a particular release of the product, the roadmap should indicate in very good detail the items covered by the release and what features may be coming up in a short amount of time. This is what we call *high fidelity near view*.

Some stakeholders may be more interested in looking at the roadmap with a slightly longer timeline reference. Although they are still interested to know the items that are to be part of the roadmap, they are comfortable with a lack of specific details, and this is what we call *medium fidelity medium view.*

Last but not least, some stakeholders, such as customers who are very important industry-level players, could be more interested in what comes into the product roadmap with a long time range in mind, which would give them important inputs about the following aspects.

- Evaluation of the product roadmap against some industry or technology roadmap.

- Give indicators about the seriousness of the organization to pursue a long-term vision for the product.

- Ensure that they don't get tied into a product that could limit opportunities for future growth and expansion plans, which they may want to evaluate in a partnership mode, for instance.

It is understood that such a view of the roadmap may not offer any details at all and could very well remain abstract and at a high level, and this is what we refer to as *high level, fuzzy abstract long view.*

When we talk about fidelity in the following sections, we mean to tie these term to the accuracy with which roadmaps are being described.

fi·del·i·ty

Exact correspondence with fact or with a given quality, condition, or event; **accuracy***.*

The American Heritage Dictionary

In the context of this chapter, high fidelity implies higher accuracy and specificity that is being targeted in a roadmap. This would depend on the period over which such accuracy is being planned, communicated, and executed. In the following sections, we'll look at some aspects of this to understand the different views and their granularity through examples.

High Fidelity Near View

What does a near term view of a technology roadmap look like? What is the level of detail that is expected to be available from such a view? What is the duration such a view should ideally be meant to cover?

Let's tackle the last question first. In most cases, a near view is about the now. What are the features present in the product (manifested by the technology) as of "now"? If the product is bought now or in the near future, what should be expected from the product? Those would be the expectations to be satisfied by a high fidelity near view. Most product sheets of available products should give the high fidelity view of the roadmap. In some cases, if there is no update planned to the product in terms of a new release, the near view could even be the current feature set supported by the product.

As an example, let's look at the 3GPP technical roadmap planning for different releases starting from Rel 8—Introduction of LTE, as shown in Table 4-1 (`http://www.3gpp.org/specifications/releases`).

Table 4-1. *3GPP Roadmap Planning*

Release	Spec Version Number	Functional Freeze Date
Rel-13	13.x.y	March 2016
Rel-12	12.x.y	September 2014
Rel-11	11.x.y	June 2013
Rel-10	10.x.y	June 2011—Introduction of LTE-Advanced
Rel-9	9.x.y	December 2009
Rel-8	8.x.y	December 2008—Introduction of LTE

It is interesting to note the caveats that 3GPP places along with this roadmap information:

- After a release is frozen, no new content can be added, but protocol specifications may still not be complete—in simpler terms, the *what* part of the release may be finalized, but details about implementation may still be under work.

- Different parts of specification version numbers can be incremented for different reasons and the "y" part is only for a flawed implementation of a specification version.

Now that the roadmap items are available, one may want to look at what content is available as per Rel 11, slated to be complete by June 2013 (which will be the nearest planned release at the time of writing of this chapter). To do this, the roadmap should provide a way to obtain a detailed view of items, which 3GPP provides in multiple ways:

- 3GPP provides a detailed list of studies that were conducted as part of this release.

- 3GPP also provides a release description document that describes all changes introduced as part of the release in particular areas (e.g., *LTE features* in section 10 of Overview of 3GPP Release 11 V0.1.6 [2013-09]).

- The 3GPP specifications release version matrix also gives information in tabular format with specifications and release versions from which they were introduced. To understand items changed or introduced from Rel 11, one would have to search for 11.0.0 in the same page (http://www.3gpp.org/DynaReport/SpecReleaseMatrix.htm).

To complete the discussion in this section, we could see that the item presented in Table 4-2 is part of UTRA, LTE Features in Rel 11: 10.2. Further Self Optimizing Networks (SON) enhancements UID_530030 93. By getting into the specification information related to this, the detailed view of the same work item can be seen. As shown in the excerpt in Table 4-2, the specifications and technical reports that are related to this can be referenced.

Table 4-2. *Specification and Technical Report Excerpt*

UID	Name	Hyperlink	Status_Report	Notes	TSs_and_TRs
530130	Core part	RP-120314	RP-121557	RP#58 completed	25.331, 25.401, 25.410, 25.413, 25.423, 25.433, 36.300, 36.331, 36.413, 36.423

The detailed information of the specifications can again be fetched from 3GPP pages, and this would complete the high fidelity near view of this:

- The reason it is high fidelity is that the exact content that is to be part of any frozen releases is specified in great detail.

- Given a particular specification, it should be possible to verify the accuracy with which (fidelity) a product complies with the specification.

As an LTE solution provider, for an operator, it should be possible now to understand what a vendor is proposing if the vendor quotes compliance to 3GPP Rel 11 in some upcoming version of the product.

Medium Fidelity Medium View

Now it should be relatively easier to understand what a medium fidelity view should be covering. The duration should be long enough that it covers not just the features planned for the technology in the immediate future, but also for some time in the future. It could be argued that anyone interested in how the roadmap will affect the immediate future (of any commitments that they make) and more would be interested in a medium fidelity view of the same, covering maybe a year or more. It could vary depending on the technology and how soon the business changes roll out, of course.

The information graphic in Figure 4-2 gives an idea about medium fidelity medium view in the sense that:

- It talks about items to be worked on in the next few years (indicated, but not mentioned in the graphic).

- It also informs about some technology drivers that could be targeted (e.g., data rates up to 500Mbps speeds in uplink, 1Gb/s with low mobility, support for bandwidth of up to 100Mhz).

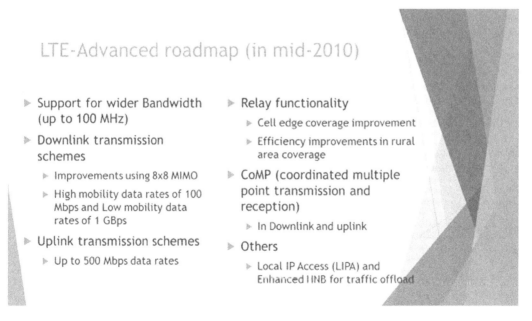

Figure 4-2. *Medium fidelity medium view roadmap example*

It should also be noted, however, that some of the items indicated in the medium view will overlap with the low fidelity view as they are describing the same roadmap in different ways and would depend on the viewpoint of the reader.

Low Fidelity, Fuzzy Abstract Long View

As a standard roadmap view, any single picture or graph that tries to capture all of the information to be made available in a technology roadmap across different years tends to give a low fidelity, fuzzy abstract long view. The following observations of such a view will make things clearer before we revisit the same with an example:

- The duration covered by such a view could very well be a few years or more (like the next decade).

- It is low fidelity, as the accuracy associated with the items listed, being part of the actual technology down the line, is also pretty low.

- During such long time periods, it should be observed that the roadmap will have items that have more to do with forecasting and speculative positioning than what the markets and consumers would be wanting at those time periods.

- It is also clear that the expected commitment level to the items listed in such a view is pretty low. Hence, it would not be a surprise if items listed in a five-year plan do not actually make their way to the technology in those five years.

The roadmap in Figure 4-3 from 3GPP is one such low fidelity roadmap view, which gives a summary of how different features were introduced over the years and gives information on what is planned for the next two years (at that time, in 2010).

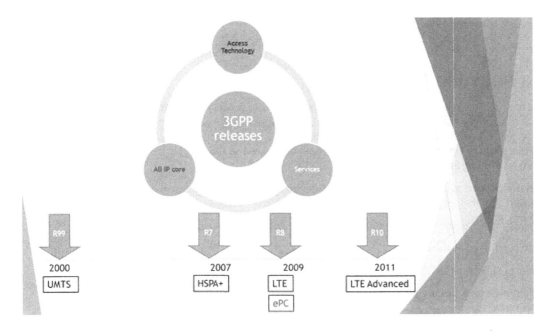

Figure 4-3. *Example of a low fidelity long view roadmap*

The high level view shown in Figure 4-4 gives more information on how the network capabilities are intended to evolve over time. Although it does not give much information on exact timelines, it is interesting for the discussion here. One can see here that speeds of 1000Mb/s are planned to be achieved in the roadmap, with LTE-Advanced in the future.

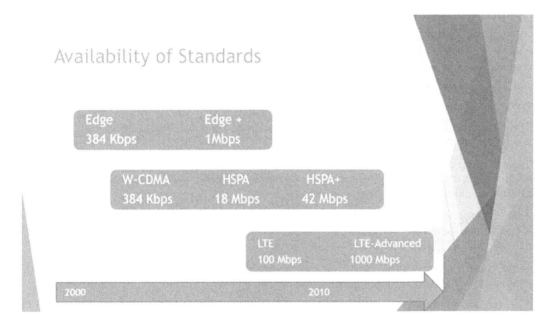

Figure 4-4. *Example of a high level view roadmap*

What Is a Network Roadmap?

Briefly stated, a network roadmap provides information about how a network is planned to evolve over time, from a given position, referenced by various attributes that comprise the aspects of the network under evolution, so that a set of goals could be met or a vision for the network could be achieved.

The items that could be covered in such a roadmap could vary based on the network under discussion and the organization that is planning the roadmap, as in:

- Physical aspects of the network, such as the different network elements that make up the network and their capabilities

- Characteristics of the network performance

- Services offered by the network

- Users or subscribers of the network

- Different devices that are supported by the network and their capabilities

- Aspects of end-user visible performance of the network like, for example, user-experienced speeds in downlink and uplink for an operator deploying an LTE network

- Implementation aspects of the network, such as the transport layer and whether the transport will be ipv4 or ipv6

- Nonfunctional aspects of the network, such as security, availability, reliability, or administration

- Ability of the network to integrate with other existing networks

Before we go any further, let's look at a small illustration of a network roadmap, courtesy of the Georgia Tech Research Network. Although the roadmap itself was published in 2010, what is of interest here are the elements that are visible. The roadmap itself is accessible at `http://www.oit.gatech.edu/initiatives/network-roadmap`.

The guiding vision for the network is explained (excerpted below) so it is easier to understand the context in which the roadmap and the items under progress are presented. For any organization, it is important to have a clearly defined vision for the network itself, even if this is also expressed in terms of business goals.

> *[T]he purpose of the Georgia Tech network has been to provide a strategic resource and sustained competitive advantage to the Institute as an educational and research enterprise, and to our faculty, students, and staff. For the last two decades, Georgia Tech and OIT have provided instrumental leadership in regional, national, and international high-performance networks for research and education.*

Office of Information Technology, Georgia Tech, Network Roadmap 2010

The current status of the network is summarized later, and this is also an important aspect. Before the future proposals for the network can be understood, one should know where the network stands currently in terms of scope, connectivity, and operations status.

Also an executive summary is made available to explain the overall directions for the roadmap. This is important in multiple ways:

- The summary provides a high-level view of items that are taken into consideration for making the roadmap.

- Without getting into too much technical detail, the reader could get an overall picture of the roadmap directions.

- The summary could also help the reader understand that not all goals expressed are actually planned to be achieved in the same roadmap duration, and some goals could be achieved through multiple steps (when the detailed roadmap is perused).

The "Executive Summary Overall Direction" from Georgia Tech states:

> *Network expansion and enhancement to reflect the state-of-the-art and to accommodate the Institute's strategic goals and developing academic, research, and business needs*
>
> *Focus on faculty and research enablement*
>
> *Enhancements in disaster recovery and redundancy options locally and globally*
>
> *Network and firewall equipment refreshment on a 5–7 year cycle*
>
> *Wireless network coverage throughout the entire footprint of our campuses, indoors and outdoors*
>
> *Leveraging of automation, scaling, self-service, monitoring/measurement, and change management*
>
> *Proactive evaluation and implementation of best practices and technologies for network integrity*
>
> *Evaluation and piloting of new technologies in preparation for future deployment, needs, and opportunities*

From this summary, we can discern multiple items that will be emphasized later in terms of generic influences on a network roadmap, such as:

- Fundamental purpose of the network to achieve the institute's strategic goals

- Key functions like faculty and research enablement

- Nonfunctional requirements (disaster recovery, redundancy) that are covered

- Directions on network coverage for the campus

- Network management and monitoring abilities

- Security aspects of the network and equipment (firewalls)

- Ongoing activities to evaluate and pilot options

The roadmap itself, with activities planned for the network, are mentioned in bar chart format in terms of the actions and timelines, as excerpted in Table 4-3.

Table 4-3. *Planned Activities for a Network*

FY2010 GOALS: (Partially Funded)	1Q FY10	2Q FY10	3Q FY10	4Q FY10	1Q FY11	2Q FY11	3Q FY11	4Q FY11
Increase to 75% deployment of 10/100/1000 to the desktop	■	■	■					
Increase to 60% deployment of 10GigE to campus buildings			■	■				
Network Admission Control (NAC) pilot (802.1x) for campus networks		■	■					
Ongoing IPv6 pilot for campus networks with improved services and performance	■	■						
Next generation firewall technology evaluation and pilot	■	■						
Multicast deployment to campus networks		■						
DNS upgraded to distributed anycast servers; transition to distributed Bluecat appliance infrastructure	■	■						

Excerpted from Office of Information Technology, Georgia Tech, Network Roadmap 2010

So it can be seen that as an organization, the definition of a network roadmap and keeping it up to date and alive could play a very important role in meeting business objectives and making all stakeholders aware of how progress on the roadmap is being made.

Also as an LTE operator there are a wide range of parameters to think about and plan for the network at the macro level. When we discuss parameters, we do not mean the deployment and fine-tuning parameters that we discussed in earlier chapters, but rather the higher-level options that could help to better plan the network for the operator.

Network Options

Why should an operator consider network options as part of the roadmap strategy? The very simple answer is that finding options in the network gives the operator more leverage into the network realization and multiple paths to achieve the business goals. An example is provided in Figure 4-5.

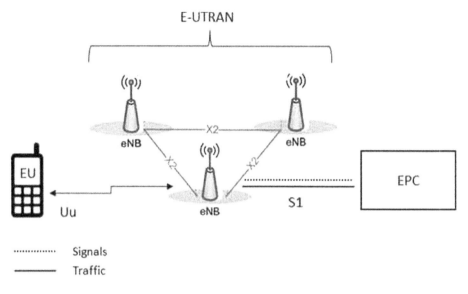

Figure 4-5. *Aspects of network flow*

Under network options, the following aspects need to be given due consideration:

- Aspects related to physical network in terms of the air interface:
  - Bandwidth to be deployed
  - Access technology being used (FDD/TDD)
- Aspects related to the eNodeB being deployed, as in:
  - Cells supported by the eNodeB
  - Antennae and MIMO capabilities of the eNodeB
- Aspects related to interconnections between the eNodeB:
  - Ability to implement X2 interface
  - Effectiveness of the radio resource management algorithms
  - Additional capabilities related to self-management of the resources such as SON (like) capabilities
  - Support for handovers for the user equipment with other networks (3G, 2G, etc.)
- Implementation options for the ePC:
  - Whether multiple physical nodes are implemented to support MME: security gateway (SGW), and packet data network gateway (PGW) nodes
  - The kind of roaming access is supported and required for the network in question
  - How the protocols S1-C, S1-U, S5, S6, S11 are implemented

- User equipment classes and types to be supported:

    - Devices that consume the LTE service and nature of mobility

    - Definition of different types of users to be supported

Note Some aspects related to the user equipment and types of users also overlap with the definition of usage models, as explained in the section below.

Deployment Options

Under deployment options, the operator must meaningfully think about actual steps by which deployment could proceed. Hence, it could make sense for the operator to mull the actual sequence of deployment over time, or with the physical necessities of deployment in terms of coexistence of the solution with other existing options and avenues for the targeted consumer.

The following are some options that could be exercised by the operator:

- Positioning of the network in terms of size, as in Macro, Pico, Micro, or Femto cell network

- Number of users supported by the network as capacity during different phases so the investment need not be huge upfront

- Coverage planning for the network:

    - Will it be a greenfield (fresh and independent) network?

    - Will it be deployed as an overlay with other existing 3G or 2G cells?

- Locations that will be deployed first as part of a deployment strategy:

    - Will a tough location with lots of users and variable traffic be chosen as the first cell location to help understand the ability of the system to tackle load and observe system performance degradation?

    - Will easier locations with not too very challenging capacity or system dynamics be chosen to start deployment, to help tune the network parameters before venturing into tougher and more demanding cell locations?

- Services supported by the network:

    - Will all services be enabled from the start or will the deployment start with the most important business essential services and branch out to other additional services later?

    - Will certain services be supported in one's own network like VoLTE or will initial deployments support voice by handing off to other networks to enable staggered investments?

- Will operation and maintenance components be enabled from the start and what capabilities from the following will be enabled and when?

    - Logging and monitoring of service availability

    - Remote management of network elements, including automatic restart and reconfiguration

    - Automatic system performance tuning

Usage Models

Every operator has to invest considerable attention to how the elements of users, services, subscriptions, applications, and traffic shape up in the network that is being deployed. Defining models of usage for the same and the key performance indicators (KPIs) of the network with which they are tracked gives the operator much needed information and a framework to analyze directions intended for the network and assess performance of the same.

In the category of devices, the following classification could be used:

- Handheld devices

  - Smart phones

    - With or without touchscreen and usage with data, applications

  - Basic phones

    - With voice only and basic SMS capabilities

  - Tablets/Phablets

- Laptops

  - With integrated modems (internal)

  - With external modems (USB based)

  - Using smartphones as modems for access to network

Mobility of the devices could also determine usage patterns, as in:

- Access with no mobility (fixed laptops)

- Access with limited or localized mobility (within home or small areas)

- Access with low mobility (mobility in a car or low-speed transport, including by walking)

- Access with high mobility (higher speeds of travel, implying more complicated processing requirements from the network)

Communication channel end points could be based on entity-dictated aspects of the processing, as in:

- Person-to-person communication (voice, SMS, MMS)

- Person-to-machine communication (online banking, entering data via phone)

- Machine to machine communications (phones registering for location updates, analytics and data collection, traffic monitoring applications)

This is also important in profiling and modeling of usage based on the types of applications being used, as in:

- Social applications (presence, Facebook communication, notifications, Twitter)

- Gaming (online and multiplayer)

- Business applications (VPN, online applications, corporate network applications)

- Voice and multimedia communication applications (voice conferencing, video conferencing, chat)

- Entertainment (music, movies, video download)

- Personal e-mail

- Instant messaging

- Content sharing (photos, video, music, file upload)

- Search services (location based content, need-based search, directories)

KPIs need to be defined and tracked so as to understand the impact on the system due to the above-listed reasons and these may be:

- Tracking of resources: acquire, usage, and allocation:

    - Physical layer resources

    - Network layer resources

    - Core network resources

- Turnaround time from the initiation of a request to the network and completion of the same

- Mobility statistics

    - Time taken for location updates

    - Number and types of location updates

- Handover statistics

    - Number of handovers initiated and successful

    - Classifications for failures and reasons

    - Time taken for handovers

    - Service disruptions caused during handovers

- QoS monitoring of:

    - Admitted bandwidths against actual provided bandwidths (how much of the ensured requests were processed successfully)

    - Requests for downgrading or upgrading of bandwidths (how many users and services were needing updates)

    - Maximum bandwidths allocated against actual usage (how many resources are being used per allocation)

    - Servicing of users based on priority

        - Gold class users (highest priority premium users)

        - Silver class users (medium priority users)

        - Bronze class users (lowest priority users)

What Influences Network Roadmap Planning?

In the preceding section, we briefly investigated network options that could play a role in evolving your network roadmaps. Also, we saw different deployment options that could determine how the roadmap gets solidified. Finally, we also saw aspects of usage models that need to be understood to visualize how the network roadmap can be analyzed and how different data points could be tracked in terms of performance indicators necessary to determine the current and future path of network roadmap evolution.

This section will explain the influences on the network roadmap from different perspectives. We will explain the impact on the roadmap from key stakeholders' perspective and how they may influence the roadmap. Also, we will also examine factors that influence the roadmap in terms of technology, usage, among others. Then we will discuss disruptive factors that need to be factored in to make sure that the roadmap does not suffer from materialization of such risks.

Key Stakeholders for Roadmap Inputs

The initial sections of this chapter discussed technology roadmap planning. From that you learned about the need for a technology roadmap, methods by which it can be evolved, and the different levels of visibility a roadmap could provide to satisfy expectations for different stakeholders. This section examines the impact of stakeholders on network roadmaps. We will explain the motivation of each of the stakeholders and how they influence the roadmap planning. This section should prove useful to help you understand the complexities of roadmap planning and to factor in inputs from such key stakeholders and manage their expectations.

Business

Business ownership normally rests with people responsible for business development in the company. These would be those who are entrusted to have an innate understanding of the product domain and the market. They could be from marketing, sales, or from product line management. Also, they are likely to be knowledgeable of different trends in different markets as targeted by the company with their product.

■ **Note**   It should be clear as to who has the responsibility for business ownership for your product. It is always a good idea to make this explicit, even in cases where the responsibility may be distributed.

What kind of inputs could one expect from such business owners that could influence the roadmap planning? Broadly speaking, the business owner may have inputs to the roadmap based on following lines:

- Business development plans
- Proof of concepts or demonstration inputs
- Inputs on end-of-life decisions
- Portfolio development decisions based on investment plans
- Inputs on timing of particular releases

Business development plans are normally based on how the product is placed and performing in different markets. To move a product from an established market or geographic area to newer markets (which could even involve newer countries or continents) may require certain specific features to be addressed by the product. For example, one decision could be that the network roadmap necessarily needs to involve support for a TDD duplexing method to be able to deploy it in a large market like China. Even in this regard, it is the duty of the business owner to clearly define the scope or extent of the feature support required within a definite timeframe to make the business plan fruitful.

Many sales and marketing ideas meet with customers' needs and are sometimes planned based on demonstrating the capabilities of the product. Although in many cases this implies a demonstration based on existing capabilities of the product in the current network, in many cases increasing it implies showing some proof of concept of a certain feature. Although the feature may not completely work as per the field definitions, it would be defined to show some capabilities of the feature in question to convince the customer about capabilities of the product. Business inputs about when such proof of concept demonstrations are needed are vital to the network roadmap. Also, in the telecom industry in particular, many product launches and feature demonstrations are planned to be unveiled in noted symposiums attended by vendors and customers alike. Businesses should give input about which features are planned for such demonstrations so they can be part of the network roadmap. For example, every year, many product launches are planned for the Barcelona Mobile World Congress held in Spain. So the network roadmap must be planned to incorporate development of the feature to be ready in time for the planned demo.

When it is time to stop supporting some features or options for the product, this call should come from product management. Businesses should assess the impact of not supporting a particular feature in terms of the effect on the customer base and actual usage. It is also the onus of business development to communicate such decisions to key customers and ensure their acceptance is received. It is most likely that such end-of-life decisions will be turned into opportunities to push support for newer platforms or upgraded features by product management when they interact with customers, old and new.

Typically, organizations get a limited amount of money as a budget to work their business plans. Deciding how this budget will be allocated for product development and which features get prioritized into the roadmap is a call the business has to make. It is the prerogative of the business personnel to work out the return on an investment and align the decisions to the overall strategy of the company for that particular planning year.

Also, as discussed previously, business development also has a say on when major milestones get planned in the roadmap. This may include deployment of new features on the network or the availability of new releases to the customers. This could also include timing of some upgrades for customer networks. A primary reason for this could be to ensure business commitments for some customers that are met within certain quarters so the revenue from the customer can be recognized for the same idea. This would help align the product with financial goals to be achieved by the company and help to meet or exceed them.

In summary, business development personnel play a critical role in roadmap planning and implementation. They need to be properly represented in roadmap development and need to have an active say in the decisions that are made. The profitability of the product is owned by business stakeholders, and ensuring their representation and involvement goes a long way in making sure the roadmap helps the product and, in turn, helps the company deliver value in a planned manner.

Customers

Some skeptic may ask whether customers really need to be involved in the roadmap development. Some of them may be doing so armed with the following seemingly valid line of reasoning: It isn't our job to learn how business development is supposed to interact with customers and ensure their requirements are properly represented. If business development does its job well, why would we need to get customer representation and interaction as part of the roadmap planning?

Even when business development represents customers, it is good to maintain focus on specific requirements from customers and record them in such a way that when the roadmap gets enhanced further, these inputs act as markers to ensure the customer input does not get invalidated.

One of the prime reasons for this is that, depending on the size of the product and time taken for roadmap development, which may again depend on the number of stakeholders involved, we may be talking about a process that could take from weeks to months to complete. In such times, when customer requirements are not properly represented, some of them may get overlooked in further development. It helps to make explicit note of certain customer commitments that need to be fulfilled by the roadmap and also to ensure that when decisions need to be made in between the selection of features for the roadmap, these customers are kept apprised of the impact.

Primary inputs from customers for roadmap planning include mainly the need for specific features to be deployed to help customers meet certain requirements. For example, support for E-TM Transmission Mode self-tests may be needed to meet regulatory requirements.

In addition to these features, however, additional customer input, as list below, is also quite important to ensure that the roadmap covers all of the necessary aspects required by the customer. These could also be considered indirect inputs for roadmap planning, which could help explain the gaps in this information and also help tune the plan:

- Specific requirements toward quality assurance of the product and the network. This may depend on the kinds of interoperability tests customers expect the product to go through. This would need to be planned in product development or in early customer testing.

- Time taken toward integration of the product with all equipment at the customer's premises so that product releases can be planned in time for demonstrations that need to happen on specific dates.

- Specific interdependence and interoperability requirements toward hardware and software components the product needs to work in the customer's networks; support for these needs to be planned in the roadmap.

- Roadmaps that the customer shares with their end users, where available, would provide good input for planning the product's roadmap. This would help the product go beyond meeting what is stated to be customer's input, but also help ensure the customer's needs are satisfied.

These steps could be made to work where there is one customer or a few major customers who are primary recipients of the product under development. What could be interesting though is if the product is positioned in such a way that it is planned to be used by a set of users who are too numerous to be targeted individually in the manner described to collect their inputs. How are inputs to be collected for roadmap development in such a scenario? In fact, many products may fall into such categories where they have the distinct need to target possible customers who may not even be signed up for the product.

In cases where the product has a wide variety of users to cater to, it would be valuable to do end-user modeling. Such user categorization could then be used to associate with specific requirements or features that are part of the roadmap, which can be recorded in the form of user stories or use cases or user scenarios. Users could be modeled in terms of:

- Usage profile of the product (e.g., in terms of amount of data used)

- Applications used by the user (e.g., business and corporate applications, home entertainment)

- Age profile of the users

■ **Note**   Some inputs related to user categorization can also be derived from the discussion earlier in this chapter where product usage has been covered in more detail.

Another way of capturing enough end-user input from customers is by using the technique of customer representatives or customer surrogates. As part of roadmap development, one could have representatives for customers or for specific customer roles and gather inputs from these. These could be real people who are playing roles of customers from outside the product organization. Business representatives could also play the roles of customer surrogates to ensure that they provide valid and vital input that could be required to finalize the roadmap. These sessions could provide frames of reference for certain features as well as answer some critical questions from the development organization to help develop a valid roadmap. Engagement of such surrogates could be an ongoing process to ensure vital and valid input is received throughout the product development lifecycle, not just during the roadmap development phase.

Customer Support Representatives

There is yet another group of stakeholders who constantly interact with customers and who are primed to give further input to the product roadmap. These are the personnel who perform the role of customer support. Such customer support representatives bring valid input to the product roadmap in terms of:

- Issues faced by customers during different phases of the product deployment:

    - Initial deployment

    - Installation

    - Monitoring and control

    - Support for field issues

- Critical feature input that could help make successful customer deployments a reality

- Vital input from competitor products that are deployed to the customers, which could indicate parts where the current product roadmap is found lacking

- Prioritized history of key "Asks" from the customers that have not been fulfilled, the value of which may be pretty high from the customer's perspective

- Critical issues logged in the product defect log from the field as reported by customers

Customer support representatives bring a further dimension to the product roadmap apart from explicit input received from business and customers. These inputs, when channeled and triaged well, give good indicators as to how the product is performing in the field and what critical aspects of the product roadmap need to be improved to ensure greater success for the product. Ignoring such inputs could mean any of the following impacts to the product and roadmap:

- Increasing number of issues from deployments

- Deployments taking longer time periods than planned

- Increased costs of product development

- Poor customer satisfaction and hence poor customer retention

- Poor perception of product quality in the industry

- Reduced viability of entering newer markets and impairment in capability to introduce newer features successfully into the roadmap and in the field

Known Factors

This section will explain more about the impact of different known factors on network roadmaps.

Technology

When we discuss the impact of technology, we have to consider a couple of aspects here. The first is that when we consider impacts of technology, we must also consider the technology used to implement the product. The second is that the product also makes available a technology to its customers and users that should also be evaluated when the roadmaps are defined. Here, we consider the impacts in terms of both aspects on the roadmap.

Implementation technology tends to get chosen pretty early in the product development cycle and most often tends to age badly. Such technology tends to feel like an albatross around the product's neck, limiting the scope of improvements achievable in the product. The following factors could help a business know if parts of implementation technology need an overhaul:

- Are the tools used in the product development still current?

- Have any of the software packages reached their end of life?

- Are there issues seen in the field or during testing that cannot be fixed as the implementation technology inherently has these issues (or so goes the root cause analysis)?

- When new features get implemented, does development most often take more time than planned due to gaps discovered in the implementation?

- Do security scans done on the product highlight outdated packages that cause vulnerabilities in the product?

- Are there any performance requirements from customers that simply cannot be met with the current product architecture?

If your answer was yes to even some of these questions, you should consider an upgrade to the product's technology one of the important aspects in the roadmap. A business should see this as an investment in the product's development to help it achieve further success and not get crippled as newer features are developed.

Of course, overhauling the implementation technology need not be done in one all-or-nothing swoop if it is determined that it poses risks to the roadmap. The parts that make up the technology could be carefully analyzed to make a phased transition to more current technologies, in smaller increments, while making sure that the functionality that is already implemented is not broken. This needs some very careful planning and execution and would require help from the people with the best knowledge of the product and the domain to make the transition successful.

The second aspect of technology, the technology that is provided to the customers through the product, can be addressed through some of the following aspects:

- Interfaces exposed by the product to the end users, like:

    - Graphical user interfaces (GUIs)

    - Protocol-based command line or other standardized interfaces, like representational state transfer (REST) APIs

- Standards implemented by the product:

    - Standards as prescribed by 3GPP, ITU-T

    - Other RFCs for specific parts like implementation of session initiation protocol (SIP)

- Operational procedures required to:

    - Install

    - Update

    - Upgrade

    - Troubleshoot the product

All of these aspects should be evaluated against expectations; not only those that are explicitly stated in the requirements, but also those that are implicitly required by customers and other stakeholders to be part of the product. Inadequacies should be addressed by the product roadmap to make sure the product stays competitive.

Financial

As connected as our world is today, finance plays a big role in impacting business decisions. Financial markets are all linked together globally to make every event of importance a global one. Investment climates tend to get very gloomy in such scenarios. This in turn would imply that global recessions are periods to be noted with great interest by business owners. During global meltdowns, decisions to buy are delayed or canceled. A roadmap needs to accommodate the impacts of such financial situations to account for possibilities of network rollouts getting delayed, plan for contingencies where dependent and supplies may be impacted, and take into account that revenue realizations may be delayed.

The company's financial health also affects the product development and, in turn, the roadmap. Financial health as measured by the cash on hand of the company is an indicator that customers would be interested in knowing. Depending on the money associated with an account, the company should be convinced it has enough capital to manage the requirements of the contract. In turn, the contrary also holds good. Poor cash position of a company could imply that some business opportunities are lost. This in turn affects the roadmap performance. Business owners tend to be cognizant of such positions and ensure that the cash position of the company is in alignment with the roadmap planned.

Geopolitical

There are also geopolitical issues to consider. To understand this better, we make a few introductions and also attempt to associate some of the recent events to the same.

Ge·o·pol·i·tics

Noun

A combination of geographic and political factors relating to or influencing a nation or region.

American Heritage Dictionary

Ge o pol I ti cal

Adj

(Physical Geography) of or relating to geopolitics; involving geographical and political elements.

Collins English Dictionary

The following aspects related to geopolitical influences need to be accommodated for in the planning of the network roadmap and also in terms of the impacts that they may have on the execution of the roadmap:

- Political climate prevailing in the region under scrutiny, as in:

  - Threat of war breaking out. For example, the aggressive intent and escalations shown by North Korea in the fourth quarter of 2013, where there were expectations of impending declaration of war on South Korea.

  - Instabilities in the government in operation that could make acts of conducting businesses challenging.

  - Regulations and embargoes that could be sanctioned and invalidate business decisions planned to be executed.

- Formation of new nation-states and changing control over certain regions.

- With some nations, there are repeating seasonal periods of distrust and demonstration of disaffection.

- Governments could also formulate newer regulations to affect certain demographies. An example is when the U.S. government changed the norms for visa applications accepted from certain regions like India.

- Impacts due to seasonal climatic conditions experienced in a place or region, for example, not scheduling rollouts when an area is set to experience seasonal storms.

Regulatory

Regulatory aspects that could impact the roadmap include the following:

- Requirements introduced by the government to which products and roadmaps must adhere. For example, mobile towers should control their radiation levels to be within certain regulatory limits. Hence, the network roadmap should not only accommodate to functionally operate within the desired levels, but also allow for monitoring and reporting of the emission levels of the product.

- Features required to be deployed as per provisions in some contracts as conducted by the service providers.

- Requirements to be able to support call tracing and lawful interception if so required by government agencies.

- Earthquake and tsunami warning system may be mandatorily regulated in a place prone to suffer the same calamities, such as in Japan.

The network roadmap would need to incorporate input related to such regulatory requirements to be able to remain current and valid.

Standards

Impact on the roadmap from standards is very direct and straightforward. The standards define the features that need to be supported to conform to a release and hence give direct input to the roadmap. As explained previously, standards' bodies are driven by different groups involved with different aspects of the technology.

Hence, by participating in the technology definition, companies can make a stake for future business revenues from implementing these features. Also, for the same reason, organizations tend to push features that are developed with lesser cost in their product into the standards to make them mandatory for competitors to catch up to. Developing features in the product roadmap before they become part of standards could be beneficial in driving home competitive advantage to the product and company developing the same.

Disruptive (Risk) Factors

All projects are subject to risks. All businesses are also operating under a set of risks. Risks could be positive or negative. A positive risk could actually be turned into an advantage to the project and help the project benefit from it.

■ **Note** The Project Management Institute has a very good set of guidelines on risk management as a knowledge area for those more interested in a detailed study of the topic.

In the context of roadmap development, a positive risk could be allowed to develop and occur. This would help accelerate the roadmap implementation or multiply the business benefits that are associated with the roadmap. More commonly though, roadmaps are subject to negative risk factors, some of which we explain briefly below.

Disasters

The United Nations defined disaster as:

A serious disruption of the functioning of a community or a society. Disasters involve widespread human, material, economic or environmental impacts, which exceed the ability of the affected community or society to cope using its own resources.

The United Nations Office for Disaster Risk Reduction

Disasters could be categorized into the following types:

- *Natural disasters*: These are events categorized as acts of nature, such as floods, tsunamis, earthquakes, landslides, among others. They could have a primary impact via the natural occurrence and they could also have a secondary impact due to damages or situations caused by the natural disaster. The 2004 tsunami triggered in the Indian Ocean by an undersea mega thrust earthquake is one such example of a natural disaster, affecting Asian countries of Indonesia, Sri Lanka, India, and Thailand.

- *Environmental emergencies*: These include widespread impact caused on the environment due to technological or industrial accidents, including use and transport of hazardous material. Examples of this include the Deepwater Horizon oil spill, which began in the Gulf of Mexico, following the explosion and sinking of the Deepwater Horizon oil rig.

- *Complex emergencies*: These involve situations of civil unrest and breakdown of governance or authority, including situations of war and political uncertainty. We have covered some of these earlier in the chapter.

- *Pandemic emergencies*: These include situations of rapid spread of infectious diseases that affect population, livelihood, businesses, and economies in some cases. For example, the H1N1 swine flu and the avian influenza or bird flu caused widespread damage to poultry, livestock, and human population. Impacts have been seen on businesses, livelihoods, poultry export, and tourism.

Disasters tend to have multiple levels of impact in terms of timelines, starting from the immediate effects on the aftermath of the disaster to long-ranging issues that last for years and decades in some cases. Disaster risk management is defined as:

The systematic process of using administrative directives, organizations, and operational skills and capacities to implement strategies, policies and improved coping capacities in order to lessen the adverse impacts of hazards and the possibility of disaster.

The United Nations Office for Disaster Risk Reduction

Let's look at what kind of influences to consider in order to accommodate such disasters into the process of roadmap planning:

- *Disaster contingency planning and impacts to planned deployments in the roadmap*: Roadmap planning can take into account probabilities of disaster occurrences and put in place a contingency plan for these. This plan could possibly include an agreed upon set of steps to take into account if a disaster materializes, including roles and responsibilities of personnel.

- *Operational implications during disasters*: Networks need to be resilient to handle operations during disasters when parts of the network may be affected or are completely out of service. Enough planning and thought should be given to ensure resiliency of networks in such scenarios and to develop the ability to provide full or impaired functionality to customers during disaster impacted times. These could include the ability to do intelligent routing, selective service prioritization, and choosing reliability over high performance.

- *Ability to support georedundancy in the product*: Geographic redundancy is the ability to seamlessly switch functionality from one or more parts of the network to other redundant parts of the network so end users of the system face minimal to no impact in functionality. Although this is a complex feature that depends on the complexity of the network and different types of nodes being deployed, when planned and implemented well, georedundancy could be a killer feature in highlighting the advantages of the product over other rivals.

- *Early warning systems*: Network roadmaps could be adjusted to accommodate features of an early warning system as required by customer or business inputs in accordance with standards.

- *Backup and restore*: In the event of disaster, how would parts of the network become operational again? What information needs to be saved by the system to be able to re-create the necessary service? Would the system be robust enough to recover operations and also allow for the restored system to be controlled via configuration and input to selectively recover operations? Roadmaps could incorporate features that support required functionality, ensuring support for backup and restore at the levels required by the network.

- *Redundancies at different levels*:

  - *Power redundancy*: How does the network use power? What sources of power are used? How long will the system operate if there is a power failure? Should improvement to this be considered as part the network roadmap? What would be the cost of such improvements?

  - *Hardware redundancy*: What happens to the network nodes and operations in case of hardware failure? What are the impacts of failures of different units and how does the same impact end-user-visible functionality? One could use techniques like failure mode effect analysis to assess impacts of different failures and which failures need to handled as part of the roadmap.

Cyber Attacks

Security is worth lots of money. Any transaction that passes through any network is susceptible to many attacks. Some of these data are directly related to financial transactions, including bank and business transaction. Securing such data implies financial security. A secure network has many implications:

- It implies customers do not fear for personal data

- Secure networks ensure e-commerce transactions can be done without fear

- Secure networks enable financial transactions, including money transfer to be made

- Secure networks translate to more productivity for users as they need not complete operations and transactions by physically being present in some place

From the data presented in the 2012 workshop on Economics of information security, the following are the chief cyber crimes committed:

- *Online banking fraud using malware*: In a malware attack, malware is used to capture banking passwords, account numbers, and related data to get into the online banking accounts, after which the criminals proceed to steal money.

- *Online banking fraud using phishing*: In a phishing attack, criminals impersonate legal websites and create legally sounding entities to get unsuspecting users to share their personal banking information, including login, password, and account details.

- *Other forms of online fraud*: Some criminals use fraudulently obtained information about services for their personal gain utilizing business services without authorization and causing losses to the companies involved. For example, cyber criminals who hack and gather passcodes from conference service providers to use for their personal benefit.

The network roadmap addresses such issues and helps secure the product in the following ways:

- Run a security scan on the product to detect security vulnerabilities. Requirements for updating different vulnerabilities could be prioritized and made part of the roadmap.

- Find security glitches that affect parts of the product and incorporate planned security patches as part of the roadmap. This would require enough planning and testing to ensure that functionality and features are not impacted.

- Actively monitor new security threats and information bulletins regarding these and proactively protect and update the product's technology to ensure that the security threats are handled.

- Ensure network redundancy options are enabled to be able to route calls and functionality through alternate network nodes when some nodes have been compromised or rendered ineffective by attacks. An example would be the concept of an MME pool that helps provide such redundancy along with load-balancing capabilities.

- Ensure new features do not introduce additional security vulnerabilities.

- Engage a security consultancy to do a security audit of the product and the network, which could mean:

    - Intensive testing of the system for attacks by simulating these

    - Probing the system for vulnerabilities

    - Strengthening security of the system by reviewing password policies

    - Ensuring all protocols and communications are secure

    - Also ensuring all paper systems surrounding the product are secure

The resulting input would be features that could then make their way into the network roadmap to ensure a secure product that can withstand all threats.

Summary

We began this chapter by examining the need for technology roadmaps and how they can be formulated. We looked at different perspectives that such roadmaps can provide, and the level of detail that can be established in them.

We then looked at Network Roadmaps and demonstrated how network options, deployment options and usage models can be figured into them. We then analyzed the key stakeholders who provide roadmap input, and studied different factors influencing network roadmaps, including disruptive factors, as well.

Roadmaps are a very powerful tool to develop network capabilities in a planned manner. Developing expertise in defining and delivering network roadmaps goes a long way toward consistently deploying successful networks.

CHAPTER 5

Network Roadmap Evolution

Owing to this struggle for life, any variation, however slight and from whatever cause proceeding, if it be in any degree profitable to an individual of any species, in its infinitely complex relations to other organic beings and to external nature, will tend to the preservation of that individual, and will generally be inherited by its offspring . . . I have called this principle, by which each slight variation, if useful, is preserved, by the term of Natural Selection, in order to mark its relation to man's power of selection.

The Origin of Species —Charles Darwin

After a diligent inquiry, I can discern four principal causes of the ruin of Rome, which continued to operate in a period of more than a thousand years. I. The injuries of time and nature. II. The hostile attacks of the Barbarians and Christians. III. The use and abuse of the materials. And, IV. The domestic quarrels of the Romans.

The History of the Decline and Fall of the Roman Empire —Edward Gibbon

According to Darwin's Origin of Species, it is not the most intellectual of the species that survives; it is not the strongest that survives; but the species that survives is the one that is able best to adapt and adjust to the changing environment in which it finds itself.

'Lessons from Europe for American Business' —Leon C. Megginson

Most living things, evolution experts point out, survive and flourish due to two critical factors. First, the organism is so exceptionally designed for its environment that it continues to flourish in spite of many changes that push other organisms out of business; sharks and crocodiles fall under this category. Second, the organism is capable of changes in its genetic code to select traits and maximize abilities that give it an advantage for surviving in the environment. Such organisms that show adaptability continue to evolve and flourish. It is only natural to extend this phenomenon to organizations in comparing their origins, evolution, and continual growth in a stretch of organic thinking. Continuing on the same vein, while we could expect networks, superior by design, to survive forever, it is only logical to plan the way for which networks could evolve.

This chapter examines in detail some of the ways in which network evolution can be planned. Network resilience is one such tool that could help us understand the aspects of the network that need to be planned for toward evolution. It could also help us to deal with further changes in the industry, which could include both sudden unplanned changes and those that could be anticipated based on industry trends. As discussed in Chapter 4, careful planning and alignment of future goals and services would help businesses and organizations to evolve in the best manner possible.

Later in this chapter, we'll also look at organizational factors that could keep the network viable and operational. This would include having response teams in place for any contingency in the network, making detailed and careful service and business continuity plans and executing them, and the ability to infuse radical thinking into the organization to help embrace changing scenarios and anticipate evolutionary requirements. We also discuss ways to measure the mutability and agility of the roadmaps to help planners find better tools to understand and track roadmap evolution.

The primary goal of this chapter is to help you get a grasp on the aspects of network roadmap evolution that matter and introduce tools that could be used to assess and analyze these. This will be useful in putting in place a process for network roadmap evolution, which we will discuss in detail in the next chapter.

Planned Evolution

This section will discuss techniques of testing the resilience of the network and what the results of the testing can tell us about the network. This would expose the gaps in the roadmap and help you take steps to evolve the roadmap to address those gaps in a planned manner. Also we will explain how reactive evolution can result from sudden changes and how changes can be anticipated.

Network Resilience

What is meant by resilience? What does it take for an entity to be resilient?

re·sil·ience

The ability to recover quickly from illness, change, or misfortune; buoyancy.

The American Heritage Dictionary of the English Language, Fourth Edition

Resilience is denoted by the ability to be able to recover quickly from events or external forces that may cause disruption. A similar description is very much applicable to network resilience. Just as different things are innately perceived to have varying abilities of resilience, experts have found that networks too need to be designed and built to be resilient. In an age where all networks are interconnected and most systems run out of the network, the system is as strong as its weakest link, which in this case could be any part of the network that is prone to attacks or disruptions, both natural and manmade. Failures and faults that could cripple the network or add to downtime are most certainly going to cause huge losses to different entities in following ways:

- Loss of revenue to the business due to failures in network and penalty clauses about availability

- Loss of trust in the quality of the network's ability to survive failures and thwart future attacks

- Disruption of operations and services to operators running businesses out of the network

- Disruptions to customers and end users who may be running real-time and life critical operations from services provided by the network

With the increasing number of services and applications being hosted on the Cloud, disruptions to a network could imply denial of all those vital services and applications.

J.P.G. Sterbenz et al. define resilience for networks as follows:

> *[We define] resilience as the ability of the network to provide and maintain an acceptable level of service in the face of various faults and challenges to normal operation.*
>
> *Resilience and Survivability in Communication Networks: Strategies, Principles, and Survey of Disciplines* —J.P.G. Sterbenz et al. (2010)

Although resilience is defined based on a network's ability to provide and maintain an acceptable level of service, survivability of the network is also an equally important aspect and is defined as follows by P. Cholda et al.:

> *[Network survivability is the] Quantified ability of a system, subsystem, equipment, process, or procedure to continue to function during and after a natural or man-made disturbance.*
>
> *A Survey of Resilience Differentiation Frameworks in Communication Networks* —P. Cholda et al.

So what are the disciplines on which network resilience can be analyzed? The fundamental concept that governs the ideas within the resilience domain are driven by the fault ➤ error ➤ failure chain, as shown in Figure 5-1.

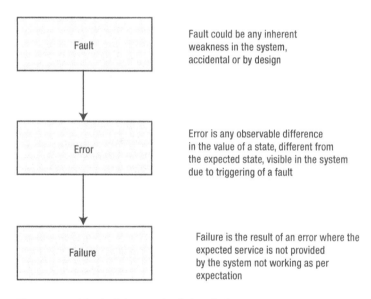

Figure 5-1. *The fault ➤ error ➤ failure link*

The rate at which dormant faults are exploited to become errors and observable errors become failures in the system can be limited by defenses built into the network. Also, by systematically improving the complete communication channel, the ability of the network to provide end-to-end connectivity to users is improved. This is disruption tolerance, also defined in following way:

> *Disruption tolerance is the ability of a system to tolerate disruptions in connectivity among its components, consisting of the environmental challenges: weak and episodic channel connectivity, mobility, unpredictably-long delay, as well as tolerance of energy (or power) challenges.*

> *Resilience and Survivability in Communication Networks: Strategies, Principles, and Survey of Disciplines* —J.P.G. Sterbenz et al. (2010)

Disciplines of Network Resilience

So how do we make the network more resilient? J.P.G. Sterbenz et al. classify the disciplines related to resilience under the following categories of challenge tolerance and trustworthiness:

- *Challenge tolerance*. As can be inferred, this relates to how the network continues to provide services on the face of challenges based on its design and engineering strengths. This could be broken down further into the following categories:

  - *Fault tolerance*: Relating to the ability of the network to be able to handle and contain fault situations from escalating to system-level issues, leading to service disruptions. Relying primarily on redundancy techniques, fault tolerance can be seen as a way of handling noncorrelated fault events of limited scope.

  - *Survivability*: A discipline that extends fault tolerance to more complicated scenarios where correlated fault events are being witnessed in the network. These could be malicious intentional coordinated efforts to bring the network down or an unintentional chain of events caused by large-scale disasters, both natural and manmade. Measures to define survivability have been suggested based on the factors drawn from *Towards a Rigorous Definition of Information System Survivability* by John C. Knight, Elisabeth A. Strunk, and Kevin J. Sullivan as a sextuple specification based on:

    - Set of acceptable service states

    - Set of service value factors

    - Reachable environmental states that the system is subject to, which normally represent the challenges for the system

    - Ordered relative service values as experienced by the user

    - Set of valid transitions that the system may make between all acceptable forms of service

    - Service probabilities that define the chances that each service state satisfies the criteria of dependability

- *Disruption tolerance:* This could primarily arise from environmental challenges that are intrinsic to communication networks. There could be a wide variety of disruptions affecting components of the network, as in:

    - Problems with channel connectivity

    - Issues related to mobility

    - Latency figures that cannot be predicted

    - Rapidly changing environment factors

    - Aspects of energy management in the end-user devices, which could mean issues with low energy levels

- *Traffic tolerance:* Primarily relates to dynamically injected traffic load into the system:

    - This could be a related to unexpected but valid events like a surge of people arriving at some location due to some valid reason (arrival of a celebrity, attending a ball game, etc.)

    - It could also be a result of attacks initiated by people or systems with malicious intent, like a distributed denial of service (DDoS) attack.

- *Trustworthiness.* Contributes a counter set of disciplines related to aspects of the network that can be measured when it is subjected to challenges. Properties related to trustworthiness give a measure of the resilience indicator of the network, including:

    - *Dependability:* A discipline that tries to quantify the extent to which a network can be relied upon to provide a service. This includes the factors of availability and reliability, which can be defined based on the following failure and repair-related measures:

        - Mean time to failure (MTTF) is the expected value of the failure density function or a measure of how soon the next failure could occur.

        - Mean time to repair (MTTR) is the expected value of the repair density function or a measure of how soon the system recovers from the failure.

        - Mean time between failures (MTBF) is the sum of MTTR and MTTF, as in the time from failure to repair to the occurrence of the next failure.

    - *Availability:* Defined as the probability that a service provided by the system or network will be operational and hence can be represented as a ratio of MTTF over MTBF.

    - *Reliability:* This is more related to continuity of service, whereas availability is more about a network being available to initiate a service. Reliability is defined as the probability of a system continuing to be in service over a defined time period.

    - *Maintainability:* The ability of the system to undergo repairs and changes to continue to remain functional.

    - *Safety:* The reliability of the system being dependable during times of crippling failures.

    - *Integrity:* This is factored into dependability in terms of the system being able to maintain its state of operations and being consistent with respect to it services.

- *Security:* This is characterized by the ability of a network or system to maintain and implement authorization and authentication policies consistently. Security is the backbone of network correctness and operation in the sense that failures in security can drastically impact other factors due to wrong access being granted to agent provocateurs and saboteurs. Factors influencing security include:

    - Authentication under security pertains to ensuring that any user of the system is indeed the same user as being claimed.

    - Authorization pertains to making sure the users are only able to perform or access services from the network they are authorized to do so.

    - Auditability pertains to ensuring that all access to the system, including success and failure, valid and invalid, authorized and unauthorized, are audited in a consistent manner and available for future review.

- *Performability:* Covers aspects of the system governing the specifications of services to be offered by the system, including the QoS aspects. Performability directly affects overall effectiveness of the network and would mostly be covered by key performance indicators, as described in Chapter 1.

In addition to these factors, the complexity of the system under analysis, in terms of the large number of interconnected systems, plays a significant role too. In a system where many subcomponents interact in diverse ways, it may be found that undefined behaviors are also being manifest in the system with interactions not in accordance to any specification. Such complexity could inherently increase vulnerabilities in the system.

Frameworks and Strategies for Resilience in Networks

This section explains the different strategies for network resilience that have been used. We then assess the importance of some recent strategies in terms of applicability to the latest LTE networks.

The Advanced Networked Systems Architecture (ANSA) project addressed aspects related to dependability in large-scale system design. Their strategy consists of eight stages: fault confinement, fault detection, fault diagnosis, reconfiguration, recovery, restart, repair, and reintegration. Performability is considered in terms of availability of acceptable levels of service.

The Alliance for Telecommunications Industry Solutions (ATIS) has developed a multilayer framework for network survivability, including four layers:

- *Physical layer.* Relating to the infrastructure available at the physical layer, including provision for geographic redundancy

- *System layer.* With representation of nodes and links between the nodes, including the ability to do switching of links based on survivability requirements

- *Logical layer.* With provisions for support of required capacity for the network on top of the physical layer

- *Service layer.* With resources required for voice and data services and having the intelligence to do dynamic routing and an ability to reconfigure to support survivability

The Computer Emergency Response Team at the Carnegie Mellon University proposes a four-step strategy, including

- *Resistance.* Covering topics of traditional security and offering resistance to threats

- *Recognition.* With tools to analyze real-time attacks and manage threat responses

- *Recovery.* Including usage of redundancy concepts and planning of contingency responses

- *Adaptation and evolution.* To manage current and future threats for the network

The Survivable Mobile Wireless Networking project introduced the following techniques for managing survivability, with a key focus on mobile wireless networks (*Survivable Mobile Wireless Networks: Issues, Challenges, and Research Directions*, by James P.G. Sterbenz and Rajesh Krishnan):

- Proposed use of adaptive and agile networking concepts where the link layers are aware of the environmental conditions and adapt to adjust operational parameters to enhance survivability, for example, selection of alternate frequencies based on feedback from channels.

- Support for routing techniques that uses geographic knowledge to enhance survival operations, such as use of alternate routing nodes when information about geographic redundancy is available.

- Adaptive networking could also include selective use of MAC (Medium Access Control) and network layer parameters to help adapt to varying communication layer requirements. For example, at some instant, ensuring correctness of delivery at lower performability regions may be the requirement, while in some other conditions maximizing throughput with low RTT could be the goal.

- Usage of satellite communication to enhance and provide connectivity in scenarios to exploit specific requirements is also part of the proposal. This includes using satellites to connect network segments that have become isolated and also exploiting specific availability and dependability windows provided by the satellite communication to be able to perform multicast operations to a large set of listener nodes for reasons of security and communication.

The ResiliNets initiative argues for a strategy based on the following axioms:

- Faults are inevitable

- Understanding normal operations is necessary

- Expectations and preparation for adverse events and conditions is necessary

- Response to adverse events and conditions is necessary

The resilience strategy of ResiliNets includes dual components: Defend, Detect, Remediate, Recover (D2R2 component), and Diagnose and Refine (DR component).The D2R2 loop, also called the inner loop, operates in real time on a proactive basis, creating defenses, applying a constant proactive monitoring of threats, remediating to actively work against an actual threat, and finally recovering to improve the weakness that actually allowed the threat to materialize.

The outer loop, also called the DR loop, works on a more long-term basis in analyzing the nature of a threat and making a diagnosis about the fundamental issues that allowed the threat to exist in the first place. The Refine action allows for a long-term remedy to improve the design, which could help eliminate the current threat and improve the ability to avoid future threats of the same category.

The Resilience Control Loop, developed by J.P.G. Sterbenz et al. (Network resilience: A Systematic Approach, IEEE communications, July 2011), builds on top of the D2R2 + DR strategy to take a system-level look at the topic of resilience strategy. It starts by defining the resilience targets and goals that are to be met. These could very well be represented system-level KPIs and other targets. Defensive measures, such as provisioning for redundancy at different layers, are prescribed, along with services that are implemented in manners in which they protect their availability. A challenge analysis component performs the role of detecting the challenges that are being subjected on the system that impair its successful working and ability to meet its services. A resilience estimator works on the information provided about the findings of the challenge analysis and makes an assessment on the impact to the resilience targets, if resilience targets are indeed not being met. Based on inputs supplied by the estimator, a resilience manager makes active management decisions to control the resilience mechanisms (including those offered by the protocols and services in the network) that are available to the system to ensure that the provided service is not impaired. It also provides further feedback to the challenge analysis on the remedy to the challenge, which is incorporated into future evolution strategies.

Reactive Evolution to Sudden Changes

A key aspect of network resilience is one of the axioms expressed by the ResiliNets framework: the ability to address the requirements placed on the network satisfactorily under all conditions initiated by establishing an understanding of the expectations of acceptable levels of service from the network. This should be followed by a thorough study of past challenges faced by the network in providing resilience. The outputs of such a study will illustrate the challenges and their impacts on resilience, including actions taken at those times and their impact on recovering the resilience characteristics of the network.

The following quote further explains the axioms mentioned previously:

> *We define an adverse event or ongoing condition as challenging (Section 3) the normal operation of the network.*
>
> *We can further classify adverse events and conditions by severity as mild, moderate, or severe, and categorise them into two types:*
>
> *(1) Anticipated adverse events and conditions are ones that we can predict based either on past events (such as natural disasters), and attacks (e.g. viruses, worms, DDoS) or that a reasoned threat analysis would predict might occur.*
>
> *(2) Unanticipated adverse events and conditions are those that we cannot predict with any specificity, but for which we can still be prepared in a general sense. For example, there will be new classes of attacks for which we should be prepared.*
>
> *Resilience and Survivability in Communication Networks: Strategies, Principles, and Survey of Disciplines* —J.P.G. Sterbenz et al. (2010)

To clarify further, this section will explain how to formulate a cogent set of steps to address those challenges that can be anticipated, their effect on the network resilience as studied and understood, and design measures that can be put in place to evolve the aspects of the network that are under stress to maintain the expected level of service.

A Generic Template

We suggest a sequence of steps to manage reactive evolution of a network. You can start by tabulating the expected levels of service, including critical attributes that could categorize the service. The KPIs of the network need to be listed, along with the service expectation to complete the understanding of requirements of network resilience. You can also mark critical KPIs among those that would necessarily need to be addressed.

Next the challenges that can be imposed on the network should be tabulated, including detailed explanations about the impact on the network, by positing impacts on the KPI and the variations that could be expected. The intent of such tabulation is to gain a critical understanding of the challenge to the network and to understand the detailed impacts on the characteristics of the network as denoted by the KPIs. It is also recommended to include past challenges that have been recorded during the operations of the network under question and how the critical KPIs were impacted during these.

The next step would be to link the critically impacted KPIs and make an assessment of the parts of the system that are unable to maintain the requisite functionality and thus impair the KPI as a service of the network. The critical components of the system should then be analyzed to understand how these can be reactively managed to address the challenge posed and to ensure that the key services offered by the network still manage to satisfy QoS criteria set on the operations.

To complete the process, the reactive changes that are necessary are then encoded as a set of steps to be triggered manually or are recommended to be built into a set of automated processes in the network that could reactively address the challenge by managing and evolving the necessary parts of the network to satisfy the operational criteria. SON concepts (as discussed in Chapter 2) include measures that address such automatic evolution decisions.

A Specific Example

One of the events that tends to affect functioning of networks is the problem of "flash crowds." Wikipedia (`http://en.wikipedia.org/wiki/Flash_mob`) defines "flash mob," which is the equivalent of a flash crowd, in the physical world as follows:

> A flash mob (or flashmob) is a group of people who assemble suddenly in a public place, perform an unusual and seemingly pointless act for a brief time, and then quickly disperse, often for the purposes of entertainment, satire, and artistic expression. Flash mobs are organized via telecommunications, social media, or viral emails.

In a networked world, a similar phenomenon can occur that may be related to the flash mob scenario: communication networks are overloaded due to many people physically arriving at a location as part of an unplanned event (from service provider perspective) or it may be related to conditions occurring online in other parts of interconnected networks that may be sending more traffic in a burst to the network under scrutiny, more commonly called a Slashdot effect, which Wikipedia defined as (`http://en.wikipedia.org/wiki/Slashdot_effect`):

> The Slashdot effect, also known as slashdotting, occurs when a popular website links to a smaller site, causing a massive increase in traffic. This overloads the smaller site, causing it to slow down or even temporarily become unavailable . . . the name is somewhat dated as flash crowds from Slashdot were reported to be diminishing as of 2005 due to competition from similar sites. . . . Typically, less robust sites are unable to cope with the huge increase in traffic and become unavailable—common causes are lack of sufficient data bandwidth, servers that fail to cope with the high number of requests, and traffic quotas. A flash crowd is a more generic term without using any specific name that describes a network phenomenon where a network or host suddenly receives a lot of traffic. This is sometimes due to the appearance of a web site on a blog or news column.

The first response in such a scenario would be to determine the impacts on the network's KPI due to such a flash crowd event, which could possibly include the following for an LTE network:

- *Availability impact.* New subscribers may not be able to latch on to the network in the area covered by cells subject to the flash crowd.

- *Dependability impact.* Existing subscribers may face diminished or unreliable service in terms of download or other operations on ongoing requests.

- *Performability impact.* Existing subscribers may face a huge drop in performance in terms of ensured speeds in the network during the event.

Some of the conditions for handling of such situations in a related domain of video service is covered by Wenan Zhou et al. Remedial actions to this in our scenario could involve the following:

- Detection that a flash crowd event has occurred in real time

- Distribution of incoming requests to other parts of the network (neighboring cells) or to interrelated systems like 2G or 3G as a fixed rule until the flash event has passed

- Reducing QoS in a planned manner across all ongoing services in the network region under the impact

- Continually measuring system performance and taking additional measures like engaging alternate service providers to share some requests based on existing sharing arrangements kept in place for such exigencies

Selection of suitable steps to be taken would depend on and be determined by the resilience management function discussed earlier, which would control the actions and help the system handle the challenge.

Anticipation of Changes in Industry

This section provides a walkthrough of what could be a dream scenario for a company with a very successful product in the industry.

> *You have a great product running successfully in the industry. Customers throng to your product and services in huge hoards. Cash registers are ringing metaphorically all the time and the company's future seems to be limitless, filled to the horizon with nary a sunset that can be envisioned and everyone in the company is living happily ever after.*

If this sounds too good to be true, it may well be. Numerous companies with the sun-never-sets attitude have had their visions broken and brought rapidly down to the *reality of declining profits* or even bankruptcy by changes happening in the industry. The focus of our efforts here is on those situations where the changes happening in the industry have caught the company or product napping.

We focus here on an example of one such drastic change as was seen in recent history within the communications industry.

The Decline of BlackBerry

Note The information in this section relates to recent events in the decline in BlackBerry's position in the U.S. smartphone market and reasons that could be attributed for the same. It is not indicative of a position on BlackBerry's future as a company or of performance of BlackBerry in other markets.

In September 2013, the company BlackBerry made announcements to the following effects when declaring its Preliminary Second Quarter Fiscal 2014 Results (http://www.marketwired.com/press-release/blackberry-announces-preliminary-second-quarter-fiscal-2014-results-provides-business-nasdaq-bbry-1833209.htm):

- Expecting a GAAP net operating loss of approximately $950 million to $995 million

    - Resulting from the increasingly *competitive business environment impacting BlackBerry smartphone volumes*, and a pretax restructuring charge of $72 million

- Announcing restructuring plans including:

    - Reduction of approximately 4,500 employees

    - Targeted reduction of operating expenditures by approximately 50% by end of Q1 Fiscal 2015

- Further roadmap updates included the following:

    - To refocus on enterprise and prosumer market

    - Offering end-to-end solutions, including hardware, software, and services

    - Reduce smartphone portfolio from six devices to four

    - With two phones targeting high-end prosumer and two entry-level devices

- Further forward-looking statements include:

    - Increasing penetration in BlackBerry Enterprise Service 10 (BES 10) with nearly 31% increase in servers installation from July 2013

    - Board continues to look at strategic alternative (Note: more on this later in this section)

Although BlackBerry may still be able to make a turnaround and reinvent itself, the decline in the company's performance is very evident. Also, some additional information on where BlackBerry was a few years earlier (year 2011) may yield further pointers as to the direction the company's results have been leading it (http://business.time.com/2013/09/20/blackberry-to-layoff-4500-amid-massive-losses/):

- BlackBerry was employing 17,000 people around 2011

- It was the proud owner of a 14% share in the U.S. smartphone market in 2011

Compare that to the following figures:

- BlackBerry had less than a 3% share of the smartphones in U.S. market in 2013

- Its total employee strength in March 2013 was 12,700, which would undergo a reduction by nearly 35%, as mentioned above

As a result of the strategic alternatives assessment mentioned in their 2014 results, BlackBerry announced a LoI (Letter of Intent) with a consortium led by Fairfax to sell and transfer ownership (`http://press.blackberry.com/financial/2013/blackberry-enters-into-letter-of-intent-with-consortium-led-by-f.html`).

It is obvious to ask the question, Where did BlackBerry seemingly go wrong? It was very much a company in good health and named by *Fortune* magazine in 2009 to be the fastest growing company in the world, attested to by earnings growing by an astounding 84% per year (`http://business.time.com/2013/09/24/the-fatal-mistake-that-doomed-blackberry/`). Exploring its situation would seem to indicate some chief reasons for its demise. BlackBerry had ridden the wave, making phones that were tuned to serve business users with its own very unique features of push e-mail, which allowed users to receive their company e-mails automatically. Also, the usage of a qwerty keyboard enabled fully functional and easier typing. What BlackBerry did not do well was anticipate the changes that were occurring in the market. Consumers (i.e., end users) were becoming the new drivers for smartphone sales. Applications were driving mobile content, and usage and lack of applications meant lack of usability and a disadvantage in comparison to other smartphones. Mobile phones were becoming full-fledged entertainment stations, with larger screens, touchscreen displays, and additional processing and performance requirements.

Apple and Google were driving the innovations through iPhone and Android mobiles and leaving the competition behind, but they were also helped by other trends. The proprietary security feature offered by BlackBerry became its Achilles' heel for regulators who wanted to monitor communication. Faster network speeds offered by 3G and 4G networks made a big pipeline available for end users to access from their phones. Push messaging was no longer a differentiator, as the new smartphones were offering the same by default.

BlackBerry has seemingly now taken steps to adapt its roadmap and is seeking to reinvent itself in the new order of things. It is ironic though that changes that need to be made in anticipation of industry trends (trend of touchscreen-based smartphones) are often delayed by such companies until the time when they see declining results. As we will explain in the next section, failure to anticipate and adapt to the marketplace changes are primary reasons why businesses start to decline. Learning this may not be so easy though, as even cultural aspects of the organization need to be evolved to get into an adaptive mindset.

Future Goals and Services from a Business or Organization Perspective

What would be the best way to accomplish planned evolution for a company? If you discount innovative streaks that could help create industry-defining, path-breaking innovations, the most common tool available to an organization would prove to be goals and services that an organization wants to provide and target. This would help the organization in the following ways:

- Establish a process by which all key stakeholders can be involved to get a shared vision of the organization's future

- Enable envisioning such a future to be implemented using specific goals and services

- Incorporate inputs related to the latest trends as seen in the industry or domain

- Make meaningful actions to be taken to be able to change as needed

Much of this has been discussed in Chapter 4. Here we will discuss the aspect of requirements from a organizational perspective in more detail, and in the process, we will define the roadmap evolution that will be discussed in Chapter 6. Yet, for an organization to be able to implement the evolution process, there needs to be much thought given to certain organizational factors, including:

- What the maturity level of the organization is

- How contingency plans are put in place

- How the company plans to manage its service and business continuity requirements

- How open the organization is to new thoughts and nurturing an ability or culture to think openly about adapting to and embracing change

The next section will discuss these areas in more depth.

Organizational Factors

So hopefully you now understand the process of planned evolution, including the models used to assess the resilience of the network, the frameworks available for evaluation, and how organizations can plan to put these processes in action to provide reactive evolution to sudden changes. You also should now know how important it is for organizations to learn to anticipate changes that come in the industry so new directions and goals can be set to help guide the organization to evolve in a planned manner and to provide a future that still holds relevance to the network, the product, and the company as a whole, which could help sustain success and ensure profitability and increase the chances for continued growth.

As discussed previously, much of planned evolution starts with defining the acceptable levels of service and putting in place a planned process for handling challenging situations where the level of service can be disrupted. The response team plays an integral part in this process.

Response Team in Place

One of the critical aspects of deployment of any network or service involves the ability to visualize how the product will work after deployment. This will involve understanding the process by which customers will deploy the product, including any qualification cycles and what is expected from the organization during these times. What levels of service are expected and provided will also depend on the type of contract executed between the entities and the service-level agreements (SLA) that are put in place.

Let's look at it from the other side. If you are an operator, what should you be looking at before deploying a network? What are the critical questions you need to ask of an organization to make sure all the pieces are in place to help make a successful rollout of the product? You could start with the following:

- What are the capabilities of operations and monitoring that are provided by the network?

- What levels of service are ensured by the network?

- Are there dedicated network monitoring centers available?

- Are there ways to do live monitoring of the performance of the networks?

- Is there a process in place to ensure that a solution is found as quickly as possible without violating any SLAs agreed upon?

- What processes are in place to ensure that issues do not occur again?

- Is there a process in place to proactively discuss the health of the network and steps that can be taken to ensure continued acceptable performance in the face of changing requirements?

░ **Note** Aspects of network operations in regard to product features are discussed in Chapter 4.

Assuming the product features are taken care of in terms of setting up appropriate operations and management capabilities, let's look at the aspects of a response team that will help the organization responsible for network operations run a successful deployment in line with customer expectations. In organizations where a network service team exists, they have the following responsibilities:

- Interacting with the network design team, or the team that would have engineered the network (in accordance with principles laid out in Chapter 1), to ensure they understand the network

- Setting up and run the network monitoring centers on a service basis

- Performing first-level analysis on any outage reported by the customer on the network

- Analyzing and assessing the root cause and taking the necessary actions to ensure services offered by the network are not diminished

- Escalating to a customer support team for issues they are not able to handle by raising an incidence report and collecting enough information and adding their own analysis to the customer incidence ticket

There should be a customer support team of experts who are the first response team to manage issues reported by customer. Their responsibilities would include:

- Being trained experts in the product and the domain

- Understanding first-level issues and what is going wrong at the customer set up

- Collecting enough information about the issue and being able to ask further questions to understand what is happening with the network

- Solving the issue for the customer or propose a workaround within approved SLA

- Escalating the incident to product engineering to be able to get a solution if they are unable to find one

There should be a critical response team to handle scenarios in which certain unplanned events may have occurred that have put performance of the network under critically unacceptable levels. These situations include, but are not restricted to:

- A natural disaster or a manmade event (war scenarios) that may have materialized to severely impact operability of the network

- Attacks on security of the network that may have created critical vulnerabilities to compromise security of the network

Such situations require deployment of a critical response team, which would be tuned to handle the situation in the following ways:

- Be authorized to take actions to help deescalate the situation

- Have enough preapprovals to help procure necessary resources and support

- Travel to the customer's location if needed to resolve the issues on an urgent basis

- Find ways to give critical responses in very short time spans

- Help reduce the criticality of the situation to an extent that normal operations, even at an impaired level, can be resumed so the case can be handed over to the regular support team

Although having response teams in place for different levels of support to the customer is a good practice, it must be made clear to personnel in such teams how these teams are supposed to interact with one another and define the SLAs governing those interactions. This would help ensure that the teams know the roles they play and are focused on providing the best possible responses to the customer and help the network achieve is best performance. Having a document detailing the process of such engagement with the customer and within the teams is a good step toward achieving such goals.

Business Continuity Planning

Previously in this chapter, we discussed the concepts of network resilience, how it is defined, measured, about the disciplines contributing to it, and the processes and strategies for managing it. As an extension of that discussion, business continuity can be defined as the ability of the business to be resilient during challenges (including natural calamities and other manmade disasters) and to continue to operate and execute normal business functions. With that introduction, let's get some definitions out of the way.

> *Business Continuity (BC) is defined as the capability of the organization to continue delivery of products or services at acceptable predefined levels following a disruptive incident.*

ISO 22300:2012(en) Societal security—Terminology

> *Business Continuity Management (BCM) is defined as holistic management process that identifies potential threats to an organization and the impacts to business operations those threats, if realized, might cause, and which provides a framework for building organizational resilience with the capability of an effective response that safeguards the interests of its key stakeholders, reputation, brand and value-creating activities.*

ISO 22301:2012(en) Societal security—Business continuity management systems—Requirements [5]

The Business Continuity Institute defines a BCM lifecycle as one that improves the overall resilience of the organization using the following good practices:

- A culture of embedding business continuity should be at the core of the practice

- A cycle of analysis, design, and implementation should form a continuous loop around business continuity

- An outer cycle of policy and program management should be used to control and determine the overall BCM lifecycle

The British Standards Institution defines its business continuity management code of practice (BS 25999-1:2006) to cover the following aspects of business continuity:

- Scope

- Policy

- Identifying critical business functions

- Developing and managing a business specific continuity plan

- Monitoring and maintaining performance

- Embedding a culture of business continuity awareness in your organization.

A business continuity management system (BCMS), a system for managing business continuity, would thus ensure that business continuity is defined and managed effectively in accordance with the context and needs of the organization. Let's investigate the requirements for implementing such a system.

Requirements for Business Continuity Management System

The ISO 22301 standards define the BCMS framework in conjunction with the well-known quality control loop of the PDCA cycle (also known as Deming cycle), which comprises the following four phases applied continuously:

- *Plan*. Where one establishes the objectives and processes necessary for achieving the goals, and hence formulates a plan.

- *Do*. Where the steps in accordance to the plan are executed.

- *Check*. Where the results are actually checked and measured to help understand the deviations against specified results. This phase was also later changed to Study to help understand that the phase is not just about measuring, but more about understanding the results.

- *Act*: Where corrective actions are taken to help act on the significant differences between expected and actual results. This should encompass an understanding of the root causes for the deviations so the corrective actions are both remedial and preventive in nature.

The guidelines necessary to determine the framework for requirements for a BCMS are:

- Understanding the organization's needs and the necessity for establishing business continuity management policy and objectives

- Implementing and operating controls and measures for managing an organization's overall capability to manage disruptive incidents

- Monitoring and reviewing the performance and effectiveness of the BCMS

- Continual improvement based on objective measurement

Having introduced components of the BCMS, let's look at the actual requirements of the BCMS as defined by the ISO standard (`http://pecb.org/iso22301/iso22301_whitepaper.pdf`). The context of the organization should include:

- A thorough understanding of the products, services, partners, channels, and relationships to understand the impact of an event that could challenge business continuity.

- The corporate policy of the organization determines the values chosen by the organization to help drive its goals and objectives.

- The business continuity policy (BCP) determines the necessary requirements for business continuity that are acceptable to the organization.

- A strategic alignment between the corporate policy and the BCP is vital for the success of the BCMS.

- A risk assessment gives information about the risk appetite of the organization, as to what levels of risk it is comfortable with.

- Identify the relevant stakeholders and their needs and expectations from the BCMS to complete the understanding of the context.

- Impacts or constraints imposed by any regulatory bodies for operation.

Leadership is entrusted with the ownership for the success of the BCMS and also the role of sponsor for the BCMS to convey the necessary importance of the BCMS to the teams. Hence, leadership will need to ensure:

- Necessary resources are available for the BCMS.

- The importance of BCMS is understood by the teams.

- Continual support is provided to help implement, execute, monitor, and improve the BCMS.

- The right people are assigned clearly communicated roles and responsibilities for the BCMS.

Planning is the most critical part of the BCMS, and it should ensure the following:

- The plan is clear and takes into account maps to the acceptable levels of service expected from the network and product.

- The plan should provide for measurability of the functioning of the BCMS.

- The plan should ensure that there are opportunities provided to review and update it as needed.

Support includes the necessary parts needed to complete the planning in terms of:

- Synchronizing the plan with all relevant stakeholders, internal and external

- Documenting the plan correctly and making proper communication regarding the plan at correct points of time

- Provision and enablement of required resources to implement the plan

Operation is the phase when the plan is put into action after considering the following inputs:

- Business impact analysis when critical processes and services and their interdependencies are identified to support appropriate levels of service.

- Risk assessment of the various events and their impacts on business should be assessed and the risks ranked to ensure systematic processing of risks. Only those risks with enough disruptive potential as determined by the policy should be handled as part of the plan.

- The actual strategy that will be used to handle business continuity challenges should be established.

- Procedures that need to be followed as part of implementation of the BCMS should be documented, including exact conditions of the disruptive event being handled, the communication protocol that should be followed to indicate the plan is being executed, the roles and responsibilities of different people involved, and awareness of factors that could impact the effectiveness of actions.

- Exercising and testing the procedures to confirm that the procedures work as expected. It also helps if the organization can assess that BCMS work in alignment with other goals of the organization.

Performance evaluation should include:

- Permanent systems to monitor performance of the BCMS

- Formal audits conducted on a regular basis to monitor and assess the performance and collect inputs for improvement

Improvement to the BCMS should include continuous processes that are set in place to keep checking the performance of BCMS against requirements. There should be a means to control and improve the procedures and guidelines to ensure performance is maintained or improved on an ongoing basis.

All of these requirements should be implemented as part of BCMS to have a system that will enable, monitor, track, and maintain business continuity at all times, especially in times of strife and disaster. Let's look at some more specific inputs related to service continuity planning, which in many ways is a subset of BCP.

Service Continuity Planning

Service continuity planning is widely seen as a subset of business continuity planning. There is a reason for this. Most organizations look at service continuity as denoting IT service continuity. This is both a necessary and important view as IT services provide the backbone for operations of most businesses around the world. BCP cannot exist without IT service continuity planning in place. The European Network and Information Security Agency has the following to say on the topic:

> *IT service continuity addresses the IT aspect of business continuity. In today's economy, business processes increasingly rely on information and communication technology (ICT) and electronic data (e-data). ICT systems and e-data are, therefore, crucial components of the processes and their safe and timely restoration is of paramount importance. If such systems are disrupted, an organization's operations can grind to a halt. If the interruption is serious enough, and no risk management planning has occurred, a firm may even go out of business.*

So how do we go about preparing for service continuity planning? What are the steps involved in this? Will the framework for BCP also work here? These are some of the questions that need answering. In most cases, we could very well apply the principles used for developing BCP and BCMS to requirements for IT services as well.

We should start by defining the key stakeholders involved in the IT service continuity planning. Although this would definitely include key people from the IT team, it would also include key stakeholders from other business units who are dependent on the IT services for their valuable input toward defining the critical IT services that need to be assessed for continuity purposes.

This should be followed by an enumeration of key IT services and the importance placed by business on continued functioning of these services during critical periods. Comprehensive risk assessment about threats to these services should be completed and the risks and the strategies to mitigate these should be documented. Contingency plans in case of failure of mitigation should also be assessed, and alternate strategies should be put in place to handle them. One such valuable contingency planning involves setting up multiple redundant sites to take over IT and business service processing in the event of a primary site going out of service.

Provisioning of Alternate Facilities

In the event that an organization's main facility or IT assets, networks, and applications are lost, an alternate and redundant facility should be made available to help continue provisioning of services and processing of information. The Office of Critical Infrastructure Protection and Emergency Preparedness of the Government of Canada refers to the following types of alternate facilities that can be provisioned:

- *Cold site*: This form of facility is the least costly method of maintaining an alternate site. The reference to coldness is in a way related to the time taken to get the site up and running from its cold or inert state. Cold sites take a maximum time to become fully operational. In terms of IT infrastructure, the site could take time to build up services to the level that the functioning site was providing before it can handle the services by itself.

- *Warm site*: A warm site could be partially equipped with required service and facilities so that it can take over the responsibilities of an active site in a short span of time, which may be a matter of a few hours. Warm sites are more costly to maintain compared to cold sites.

- *Hot site*: A hot site is the most resilient way of maintaining an alternate site. A hot site is normally completely in synch with the primary site and can take over responsibilities very much in real time. A hot site is very costly to maintain as services and infrastructure need to be brought up and maintained to be a complete and online backup for the primary site.

The site that is selected as the primary alternate should be decided based on the criticality of the services and the cost of not providing service. This could help in assessing the tradeoff between the costs incurred by a lack of continuity vs. the cost of setting up an appropriate alternate site.

Cultural Encouragement to Embrace Futuristic and Even Fantastic Scenarios

You can lead a horse to water, but you can't make it drink

English proverb

The processes described in this chapter are aimed primarily at helping an organization improve its ability to handle challenging situations. Processes are a way to achieve a shared goal: a common language to help different people understand the issues involved in a joint venture and a common path to achieve collective results. But processes alone do not guarantee anything. Processes are only as effective as the efforts of the people who are applying them. A change in processes needs to be preceded by a change in thinking in the people involved in the organization to understand the context of the change and to appreciate the reasons for implementing the change. In the event that new processes are implemented without the mindset being changed, it may pretty well end up like the proverbial horse that is brought to the water. It may snort, it may nibble, and it may stomp nervously around, but it most definitely would not drink the water unless it has a mind to do so.

The Jisc infoNet infokit on Change Management (http://www.jiscinfonet.ac.uk/infokits/change-management/) notes the following aspects are involved in any change: "Change usually involves three aspects: people, processes, and culture."

It is not enough to get only the processes right. To properly manage the change, it is as important to understand the people involved and the culture prevalent among them. Every change that is brought about inherently faces resistance toward adoption of the change. Once this resistance is overcome, it becomes easier to make the transition and implement the change. Also, in some cases, it could make it easier to understand which aspects of the culture itself need to be changed for the betterment of the organization. The onus for cultivating the necessary culture needed to inspire and evolve an organization is largely place on leadership of the organization.

Coming back to the topic of resilience and continuity of services, it should be apparent that people and personnel involved should be encouraged to cultivate an attitude for thinking about possibilities. These possibilities could be about both good and bad events that could happen and have an impact on the business and the organization. Better anticipation in problem-oriented thinking could lead to better preparedness for such situations in that all aspects of planning—impact analysis, preparation of mitigation plans, and putting such plans into action—can help the evolution of the roadmap to embrace the change.

Roadmap Mutability

mu-ta-ble

Capable of change or of being changed in form, quality, or nature

Merriam-Webster's Dictionary

Mutability, in the context of roadmaps, is important in that it provides a way to assess whether the roadmaps are capable of changing over time. It also provides a way to check the effectiveness of the processes set in place for evolution of roadmaps under various conditions.

Having introduced a reasonably acceptable definition for roadmap mutability, we propose the following as one of the ways to measure this. It is important to understand that while the concept of defining and measuring mutability of roadmaps seems important enough to us, we were unable to find specific references to this in our searches in standard publications.

How can a change be defined as completed? One way is to define conditions of acceptance to confirm that the change is definitely in place in an entity where it is being changed. It follows that implementation of the change should be verifiable by inspection of the entity and also by observations associated with the behavior of the entity in cases where the change impacts some visible behavior of that change.

If we were to define the conditions for successful change to a roadmap, they could include:

- All aspects of the roadmap are updated

- Viable plans for implementation of updated roadmap are available

- All stakeholders involved in roadmap communication have been updated about the changes

- All documentation related to the change is completed and available

- The resources necessary for achieving the changed roadmap are in place or arranged

Based on such an acceptance of a change to a roadmap, mutability could be defined as a function of the number of valid changes initiated vs. the number of changes accepted successfully by the roadmap. A lower factor of accepted changes could imply that the organization still has a ways to go to achieve better roadmap mutability in order to evolve the network and the product at a rate at which meaningful evolution could be possible.

Roadmap Agility

a·gil·i·ty

n.

The state or quality of being agile; nimbleness.

The American Heritage Dictionary of the English Language, Fourth Edition

Although the concept of mutability focuses more on the ability to change, agility is concerned more with the rate at which such a change is possible. An entity that is receptive to change, yet not agile enough, may struggle to survive through conditions that demand better agility.

In the context of roadmaps, we could define agility as a measure of the rate at which changes are accepted and implemented as part of the roadmap. We define this measure to start at the arrival of a valid request for a change in roadmap and measure the time taken for the change to be reviewed, evaluated, and incorporated as part of the roadmap.

At periods that are deemed to be critical to the network or product, it may be a valid expectation for an organization to be able to respond very quickly to change requests. Agility at such times may be the x-factor that helps a good product that is slow to respond to changes become something close to a market leader. Such agility needs a culture of understanding between the stakeholders of the product: a shared vision and singleness of purpose to make changes happen in the product and overcome their personal differences to achieve a greater goal—that of product betterment.

Summary

This chapter began by looking at planned evolution to the networks roadmap. We defined the concept of network resilience and looked at different models this. We also walked through a strategy of reactive evolution for sudden changes, illustrated with a specific example for using a suggested template. We then suggested ways in which industry changes could be anticipated. We also looked at ways in which future goals for business and services could be used as a tool to help manage evolution of the roadmap.

We then went through organizational factors that could help in roadmap evolution—that of designing and having a response team in place, on planning business continuity and service continuity aspects, and the importance of developing a culture to embracing change in the organization.

We also briefly discussed proposed measures of roadmap mutability and roadmap agility to help assess and evaluate aspects of roadmap management for the organization, which could help answer questions about the flexibility of the roadmap and the speed with which the organization evolves.

This chapter emphasized that managing evolving LTE networks is also about paying attention to aspects of network resilience, business and service continuity planning, and being responsive to changes as needed in the industry.

CHAPTER 6

A Process for Network Roadmap Evolution

Plans are worthless, but planning is everything.

—Dwight D. Eisenhower, *Public Papers of the Presidents of the United States*

Driving is not about getting the car going in the right direction. Driving is about constantly paying attention, making a little correction this way, a little correction that way.

—Kent Beck, *Extreme Programming Explained*

Product development is tough, but getting customers to pay for what they want and keeping them happy is tougher. Remaining competitive while developing the product to suit the customers' needs and running a profitable business are even tougher. A great product remains successful over the years, has good customer backing and satisfaction, and enables the company to remain profitable enough to make even better products. This requires many people (business development, systems engineering, product development, product support, management, sponsors, customers) to work well together. And yet, their efforts may not bear much fruit if other things not under its control conspire against a company's efforts.

Critical and central to all of this is the ability of the organization to develop a culture of roadmap awareness. By this we mean not just an ability to make a great roadmap, but also cultivating a sense of caring for this, to keep the roadmap alive and active, to be aware of changes that are needed, and to be agile enough to handle the changes in a systematic way, hence, keeping the product competitive and evolving. Putting a system in place would be a great way to begin developing a culture that embraces roadmap evolution. Most companies make more reactive changes to a roadmap than proactive, and changing the attitude of people involved is just as important, if not more, than establishing a process for the same.

This chapter presents a process framework to address network roadmap evolution. We have been discussing different aspects of this in the previous chapters, but in this chapter we propose processes with necessary responsibilities to handle different aspects of network evolution.

Some inevitable caveats need to be noted here. We do note that organizations may have well-established processes to handle the various aspects of roadmap evolution. Our aim is definitely not to preempt such processes in favor of the one we describe or to recommend ours over the established and successful processes that may be in practice. However, we do believe elements of the process framework described in this chapter could help stimulate you to think about your current processes and determine if any could be improved to address some aspects highlighted in this chapter.

We begin by discussing frameworks and contexts under which roadmap development could be happening. We explore in more detail the process notation that would be followed for roadmap evolution, and then present a high-level summary of this. We also detail each of the subprocesses, focusing on the what rather than the how. Some of the processes could be optional, but it is our firm belief that in considering these processes, you could make more educated decisions on how they could be used to evolve your network roadmap.

Aspects of Network Roadmap Management

This first part of the discussion presents an overall cycle for roadmap management. We follow this by discussing how roadmaps are implemented in most products. We conclude the setup with an understanding of the stakeholders involved in the road mapping process so that we can dig deeper into the framework later in the chapter.

Roadmap Development Cycle

We propose that at the highest level, a roadmap development can be modeled through the following four phases:

- *Planning phase.* Every cycle of the road mapping process starts with the planning phase, even if this is the first time the roadmap is being made.

- *Execution phase.* Once a roadmap has been planned, it needs to be executed as per the organization's execution models through programs and projects.

- *Review phase.* The roadmap under execution needs to be reviewed on a periodic basis and findings concluded.

- *Update phase.* Every roadmap review results in some updates to the roadmap, which may need to go through the planning cycle once again.

Figure 6-1 illustrates the roadmap development cycle.

Figure 6-1. *Roadmap development cycle*

Also, throughout the roadmap development cycle, the roadmap and the changes to it should be communicated to all stakeholders, internal and external, as per the agreed-to communication guidelines set up for this. This is critical to the success of the roadmap in the following ways:

- It helps share a common vision across all stakeholders.

- It enables roadmap changes to get reviewed and gaps (if any) identified.

- It helps establish buy-in for the roadmap from the stakeholders.

- It enables stakeholders to understand and help improve the road mapping process where needed.

Roadmap Execution: Programs, Projects, and Portfolios

Ideally, all of the plans of an organization to be accomplished over a timeframe make up its portfolio. This portfolio may include development in many products in parallel. For each of these products, the organization needs to define what it wants to get developed as part of its roadmap. Each of the roadmaps may then get executed through one or more programs. Each program may need multiple projects to be executed in parallel or in sequence to complete its objective. Figure 6-2 diagrams the path of roadmap execution.

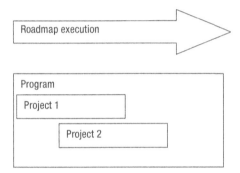

Figure 6-2. *Roadmap execution through programs and projects*

Roadmap planning must involve sound project management practices as followed in the organization by keeping the following in mind:

- Everyone should be in agreement and alignment about the roadmap execution in the near future.

- Resources and approvals must be in place for planned roadmap execution.

- Project planning should include balance for the project constraints of scope, quality, and schedule.

- Programs and projects through which a roadmap is executed must be monitored consistently with sound project management practices to be able to analyze the impacts on the roadmap.

■ **Note** We strongly recommend following project management practices as described by the Project Management Institute in the Project Management Body of Knowledge for project execution (www.pmi.org/PMBOK-Guide-and-Standards.aspx).

Factors Affecting Roadmap Development

As discussed in Chapter 5, there are several factors that affect how the roadmap gets developed. Figure 6-3 illustrates these factors. The roadmap should contain baselines as to how these aspects are addressed, and these factors also need to be continually monitored for successful roadmap development and evolution.

Figure 6-3. *Factors that affect roadmap development*

Project Management Processes

One of the assumptions that can be make in proposing a framework of processes for roadmap evolution is that the organization is already following a standard set of processes to manage its projects. We baseline our framework on the Project Management Body of Knowledge (PMBOK) framework of processes promulgated by the Project Management Institute (PMI). Hence, we assume that the processes listed in in the PMBOK framework are already part of the project management practices followed by any organization working toward roadmap evolution.

A Framework of Processes for Roadmap Evolution

In proposing our processes, we are very much in alignment with the process management framework as defined by the PMI with its Project Management Body of Knowledge. This section provides an overview of the process framework that we propose for roadmap management and evolution. Table 6-1 lists the processes and the areas they affect.

Table 6-1. *Processes for the Areas Involved in Roadmap Evolution*

Knowledge Area	Planning Processes	Execution Processes	Review Processes	Roadmap Change Processes
Integration management	Develop roadmap management plan Define roadmap	Execute roadmap	Perform roadmap review	Perform roadmap change control
Resilience management	Plan resilience management Define service levels Perform challenge KPI impact analysis Define resilience strategy		Perform network resilience review	
Operability management	Plan operability management			

Develop Roadmap Management Plan

In our framework, the roadmap management plan is the central plan that holds all the information needed to define, execute, and manage roadmap evolution as per the needs of an organization. Figure 6-4 illustrated this process.

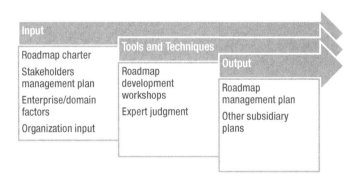

Figure 6-4. *Roadmap development plan*

Develop Roadmap Management Plan: Input

Roadmap Charter

Under a roadmap charter or an equivalent document, we expect the following input to be made available:

- Clear vision of the product or network that is to be developed with critical features and targets

- Initial input and guidance regarding key aspects of scope, cost, timelines, and other approvals for roadmap development

- Any proposals or studies done on the product roadmap

- Critical information regarding the domain or market

- Critical input with regard to chief competitors for the product and their strengths, weaknesses, opportunities, or threats analysis

- Input regarding key customers and their expectations

- Input regarding sponsors for the project and management expectations

Stakeholder Management Plan

Input about specific stakeholders and their communication requirements is needed as a basis for a roadmap management plan. Decisions need to be made about specific communication requirements from a roadmap management perspective, and these may need to override or augment the stakeholder management plan. For example, you may decide to limit roadmap communication to happen at fixed timelines in the year, while project communication may happen more regularly.

Enterprise or Domain Factors

Under enterprise or domain factors, you could consider:

- Standard input related to roadmaps as followed in the industry

- Competitor product roadmap input, if any

- Standards that could apply to the domain with respect to the roadmap under development

Organization Input

Under organizational input, you could consider:

- Processes and templates followed in the organization that could govern roadmap development

- Any specific organization level standards that could be constraining or applying to the roadmap, such as Capability Maturity Model Integration compliance

- Any other input from the organization's project management office

- Input and information from other past or current projects and their roadmaps

Develop Roadmap Management Plan: Tools and Techniques

You may find some tools and techniques are more commonly used than others. We will explain these in detail here and then only reference them in later sections when the same technique is used in other processes.

Roadmap Development Workshops

Roadmap development is a very important activity not just to decide upon the roadmap, but also to serve as a good team-building activity. We expect the following participants to be part of these roadmap development workshops: representatives from critical stakeholder groups for the product, including project sponsor, senior management, product development team, product support team, systems engineering, product validation/testing team, quality assurance team, and subject matter experts. Workshops should focus on getting consistent and valid input about how the product roadmap will be defined, documented, communicated, managed, executed, reviewed, and updated.

Expert Judgment

Although a workshop is a good way to collect input and brainstorm issues and solutions, the final decisions on the roadmap plan should be determined by expert judgment, as executed by business development personnel and approved by senior management team.

Develop Roadmap Management Plan: Output

The roadmap management plan could be a high-level document listing guidelines and referencing other plans for operations, or it could be a detailed document giving exact procedures and fine points related to how roadmaps will be developed and managed. The following critical items should be part of every roadmap management plan:

- Decisions about how the roadmap will be documented, including the following template elements:
  - Description of product or domain
  - Standards of compliance, if any, for the roadmap
  - Format of the roadmap, as in:
    - Textual representation
    - Block diagrams
    - Timeline charts vs. feature
    - Multiple levels of roadmap information
  - Configuration management of the roadmap, such as how it will be versioned and where it will be stored
  - Caveats, if any, about features listed in the roadmap and what level of confidence can be associated with them

- Guidelines about roadmap communication to stakeholders and critically to customers with information about:
  - When communication will be made
  - Who is responsible for the communication
  - What information will be communicated
  - How will customer feedback be collected
- Guidelines about how the roadmap updates will be handled:
  - Periodic updates:
    - What will be the frequency of the periodic roadmap update
    - What input will be needed to prepare for the update
    - What process will be followed to execute the update
  - Reactive updates:
    - On what conditions will a roadmap review be done
    - What input will be needed for the review
    - What process will be followed to make the review and update
- Guidelines about roadmap change board (RCB):
  - Who will constitute the RCB
  - What criteria will be followed to accept a change to the roadmap
  - What are the inputs and assessments that will be needed to perform a review
  - When and how will the RCB convene and deal with the change requests
- Data that should be collected and measured during roadmap evolution, including:
  - Data about number of times a roadmap update was requested
  - How soon the updates were dealt with
  - Roadmap execution progress
  - Recording values of roadmap agility and mutability to rate to the roadmap evolution process
- Information and guidelines about roadmap subsidiary plans (optional):
  - Operability baseline
  - Resilience baseline
  - Business continuity plan
  - Service continuity plan
  - Reactive changes plan

Define Roadmap

The define roadmap process is the main process that develops the network roadmap. The output from this process is the actual roadmap that will be executed through different projects and programs to achieve the organization's objective. Figure 6-5 illustrates this process.

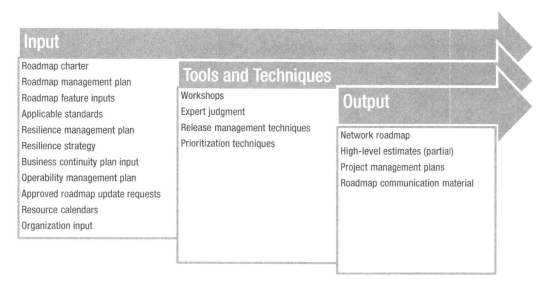

Input

Roadmap charter
Roadmap management plan
Roadmap feature inputs
Applicable standards
Resilience management plan
Resilience strategy
Business continuity plan input
Operability management plan
Approved roadmap update requests
Resource calendars
Organization input

Tools and Techniques

Workshops
Expert judgment
Release management techniques
Prioritization techniques

Output

Network roadmap
High-level estimates (partial)
Project management plans
Roadmap communication material

Figure 6-5. *Defining the roadmap*

Define Roadmap: Input

The roadmap charter and roadmap management plan are critical inputs for the define roadmap process.

Roadmap Feature Input

Features to be developed as part of the roadmap should be made available by the PLM or marketing function with the following information:

- Customer visible impact of the feature

- Motivation for the feature (needed by a certain customer, needed for standard compliance, etc.)

- Importance of the feature in terms of revenue generation capability

- Feature complexity in development and testing

- Dependency on other features

Applicable Standards

Standards that impact the features under development need to be known and understood to accurately define the roadmap. Also, roadmaps need to define the standard baseline to which they adhere, and customers use this information to understand the feature functionality, which can differ from release to release.

Resilience Management Plan

The resilience management plan should give the following input to the roadmap:

- Which resilience measures need to be developed as part of the roadmap

- Prioritized input regarding service level definitions

- Prioritized list challenges that need to be handled with information about past system behavior under challenges

- Cost or impact due to degradation of KPIs or lack of resilience handling

- Resilience input defined in terms of system aspects that could be estimated and developed as part of the roadmap

Operability Management Plan

Operability aspects of the network need to be derived from the operability management plan, including input about:

- Support provided for management of fault, configuration, accounting, performance, and security (ITU-T M.3400 standard) as per industry and organization standards

- Specific operability aspects that need to be taken care of for deployment and monitoring aspects of the network

Business Continuity Plan Input

Aspects of business continuity planning definitely impact a roadmap that is under development. Requirements for this have to be part of the defining roadmap process. However, some observations can be made here:

- In general, we consider the organization that is developing software and hardware components for the network to be the development organization. As for any organization that is operating on network development, there may be specific requirements for business continuity to be maintained. The network roadmap that is being developed may be constrained by such requirements as:

  - Developing geographic redundancy among development teams

  - Operating multiple teams to handle customer issues to satisfy service requirements

- Also, the organization that is buying the network for deployment, which would normally be a service provider, could also have specific business continuity plans under operation. These could determine the efficacy with which it can deploy, manage, and operate the network and the businesses that could run on it. These requirements should also be communicated to the PLM team responsible for customer interactions and should be included in the roadmap definition process as input.

Approved Roadmap Update Requests

Roadmap update requests that have been reviewed and approved by the roadmap change control process are input in the define roadmap process. These requests start a fresh cycle of roadmap planning for updating the roadmap that will have to be run through the roadmap development cycle.

Resource Calendars

Resource calendars provide critical input about the availability of existing resources and their competencies. It should also be clear from the resource calendars when certain resources and teams complete current engagements for ongoing projects and programs so the input is added to the roadmap under development.

Define Roadmap: Tools and Techniques

Workshops

Facilitated and focused workshops are one of the best tools to define and arrive at the roadmap. Workshops can facilitate group decision making and also help in getting buy-in from necessary stakeholders for the roadmap. The following could be implemented in workshops to help arrive at the roadmap:

- Group estimation techniques like wideband delphi could be used

- Perspectives from different groups could be shared about the importance of features and ensuing discussions could also help bring out important open issues to be noted for follow up

- Management approval and stakeholder positions can be obtained for the roadmap

Release Management Techniques

Release management techniques include making preliminary estimates for the features with impact analysis and development efforts and then slotting them into releases to understand how the features could be developed given the cost, schedule, and resource constraints. There could be company- or product-level complexities associated with the process of making a release, information that could be helpful to make a working roadmap with meaningful feature groups and priorities.

Prioritization Techniques

Prioritization techniques are helpful in ordering the features that are input to the roadmap. Different aspects could be estimated using measures like function points, story points, and so forth, and these could be used to prioritize the features for the roadmap. Dependency and interdependency between features would also need to be considered when prioritizing features. Prioritization should also take into account the value for the feature from both the business and the customer perspectives.

Define Roadmap: Output

Network Roadmap

The actual network roadmap consists of the output of the process, and depending on the organization, it could contain the following:

- A prioritized ordered feature list with links to further details about the high-level description of each feature with critical impact to the customer or product

- Input regarding release milestones, contents of the release, and the timeline for when the release is planned

- A list of which parts of the roadmap are final and which parts are tentative and could be changed

It should be a cumulative list in the sense that it should show the features and releases made in the past so the reader can completely understand and make sense of the current and future items projected in the roadmap. It should also include a list of the confidentiality clauses embedded to indicate parts that could be shared with external stakeholders and parts that should not be visible outside the developing organization (e.g., some roadmaps could make high-level estimates not visible to end customers)

The roadmap could also be under configuration control, and hence, could be named and numbered following organization policies. The roadmap could optionally include high-level estimates, areas of impact, and resource requirements for a subset of features that are of high priority and need to be part of upcoming releases.

Roadmap Communication Material

Along with the actual roadmap that is developed, other communication material related to the roadmap that need to be updated as part of the same process would be included. These could include material used by marketing teams to communicate roadmap contents at the appropriate level to different stakeholders, including current and future customers.

Execute Roadmap

We define the execute roadmap process to include execution of the roadmap through a series of projects and their releases. Figure 6-6 illustrates the execute roadmap process.

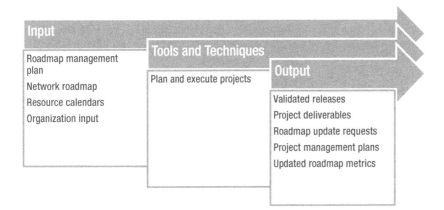

Input

Roadmap management plan

Network roadmap

Resource calendars

Organization input

Tools and Techniques

Plan and execute projects

Output

Validated releases

Project deliverables

Roadmap update requests

Project management plans

Updated roadmap metrics

Figure 6-6. *Execute roadmap process*

░ **Note**   Some organizations could choose to make project and release plans part of their roadmap, in which case they may simply execute projects to execute the roadmap. We have made the assumption that, in general, the roadmap could be developed independent of project releases initially.

Execute Roadmap: Tools and Techniques

Plan and Execute Projects

To execute the roadmap, it needs to be planned along with the projects through which it will be delivered. To make a roadmap concrete, an organization's agreed-upon horizon of features should be planned as part of the actual projects that have distinct content, timelines, resources, and a proper project plan. For example, it could be that roadmap items for the next 12 months are required to be planned in actual projects and releases and plans available for the same.

Once project management plans are available, they should be executed as per plan. As project releases get executed and validated, the actual roadmap feature execution makes progress. Agile projects that feature validation could be tracked as a feature burn down to directly map to roadmap execution.

■ **Caution** The closer project planning happens to roadmap definition, the better the success of the roadmap. Large time gaps between roadmap definition and project plans lead to stale information, miscommunication, incorrect prioritization, and ineffective products.

Execute Roadmap: Output

Validated Releases

The prime output of the execute roadmap function tends to be product releases that are validated to be of acceptable quality per the project plan. Validated releases could also be verified by roadmap owners to meet the acceptance criteria for the features that were part of the plan.

Project Deliverables

Along with executable code, which is part of the validated release, the other project deliverables are also important, such as user guides, installation guides, online help manuals, and other configurations input.

Roadmap Update Requests

When project planning is undertaken, the roadmap's concrete information that could emerge for the actual project and planning constraints may require an update to the roadmap to reflect actual project planning. This may imply that some features do not fit in to the current release and may need to be postponed or swapped with some other features. This should be formulated as a *roadmap update request* and it needs to go through the process of an update roadmap so this is reflected in the roadmap in a systematic way (i.e., taking care of other necessary items while updating the roadmap).

Updated Roadmap Metrics

Along with the execution, it is imperative to update any metrics that are collected for the roadmap management. As discussed in Chapter 5, these could include metrics like roadmap mutability and roadmap agility.

■ **Note** Refer to Chapter 5 for further descriptions of roadmap mutability and roadmap agility metrics.

Project Management Plans

We also expect the output of planning of the projects to be reflected by valid project management plans. This is necessary to ensure that the plan to execute the roadmap remains relevant and has taken into account all necessary issues to be considered while planning projects.

Perform Roadmap Review

We define the perform roadmap review process to be the critical process where roadmap execution is reviewed and necessary actions are taken to keep the roadmap current and meaningful. Figure 6-7 illustrates this process.

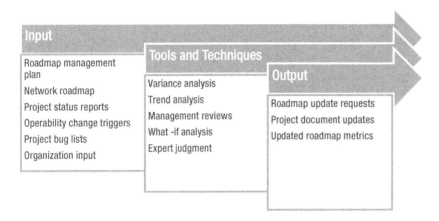

Figure 6-7. *Roadmap review process*

Perform Roadmap Review: Input

Project Status Reports

Project status reports contain important information about a project's progress. The status reports indicate items that are achieved as per plan, highlight metrics as defined and collected, and also include the input about deliverables that are behind schedule or quality and highlight risks to the project.

Operability Change Triggers

The operability change triggers are basically a periodic inputs that are collected by monitoring different operability evolution sources, as identified by the operability management plan, that act as triggers to the roadmap review. The changes to the operability aspects monitored and their impact will be quantified as part of the change triggers.

Project Bug Lists

Quality concerns that impact project completion could also be deciphered with the project bug lists, which basically contains a list of errors that are ranked as to their severity and impact to the project goals and against specific features.

Perform Roadmap Review: Tools and Techniques
Variance Analysis

In variance analysis techniques, the variance of different dimensions of the project vs. specific goals and measures is computed for different attributes. The variance is quantified and is used to take specific preplanned actions. For example, a schedule variance greater than 10% could trigger action to replan certain features.

Trend Analysis

In trend analysis techniques, a trend of an item under study is projected by capturing the data and plotting the trend against a timeline. Such a trend chart could indicate where the project is headed and could give early input to the roadmap execution and indicate concerns that need to be addressed to keep the roadmap active. For example, in agile terminology, a release burn down chart is a trend that could help with understanding the health of the release.

Management Reviews

Most organizations follow a process of review by management representatives, including sponsors for the roadmap, senior management personnel, and other functional owners who have a stake in success of the roadmap and the projects. Management reviews follow a set template in the organization where input is prepared beforehand in a certain manner and is presented during meetings scheduled specifically for that process. These reviews indicate concerns raised by management based on data presented and result in actions that could initiate roadmap change requests.

What-if Analysis

A what-if analysis uses modeling and simulation techniques to project and assess the impact of certain events on the project and roadmap execution. These results could then be used to understand the criticality and impact of project status on roadmap items and are used to take corrective and preventive actions on the roadmap and the projects under execution.

Perform Roadmap Review: Output
Roadmap Update Requests

The main output of the perform roadmap review process is requests for actual updates of the roadmap. These roadmap update requests need to go through the roadmap change control process. At this stage, these are simply changes that are requested out of the roadmap due to the review process. They are not yet validated and quantified, and they need to be critically reviewed as part of the roadmap change control process before they can be planned as part of the roadmap.

Perform Roadmap Change Control

We define the perform roadmap change control process to validate the roadmap change requests and accept those that need to be accepted as valid changes and initiated further toward replanning of the roadmap. Figure 6-8 illustrates this process.

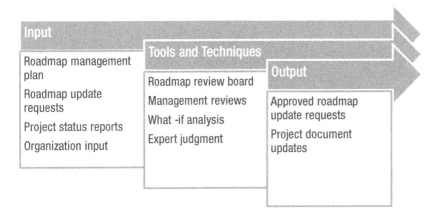

Figure 6-8. *Roadmap change control process*

Perform Roadmap Change Control: Input

Roadmap Update Requests

Roadmap update requests should have the following information:

- Reason for the update

- By which stakeholder or process the update was created

- Optional impacts or costs of making the update, including high-level estimates for project resources

- Impact of not making the update, in terms of cost to the organization, impact on customer, and so forth

Perform Roadmap Change Control: Tools and Techniques

Roadmap Review Board

We suggest formulation of a roadmap review board with key stakeholders as necessary for the roadmap and the organization with the following focuses:

- Having necessary product and domain knowledge to assess the impact of the update request

- Having enough management or sponsor representation to approve the roadmap update requests

- Meetings of the board on a periodic basis to handle pending update requests

- Meetings of the board on an ad-hoc request or emergency basis, depending on the importance of the roadmap update request

- Assessment by the board as to the cost of updating the roadmap vs. the cost of not updating

The rationale and decisions should be documented using standard agreed-upon procedures so the workings of the review board can be audited or revisited any time during roadmap execution.

Perform Roadmap Change Control: Output

Approved Roadmap Update Requests

The prime difference with *approved roadmap update requests* would be the following information that could be added during the approval:

- Detailed impact analysis for the update requests

- Details regarding the approval given and rationale behind it

- Constraints that could qualify the approval in terms of:

  - Special conditions considered

  - Limitations to the schedule window within which the approved roadmap update request has to be processed

  - Any other constraints

- Conditions under which the approval could be invalidated (if any)

Plan Resilience Management

As mentioned in Chapter 5, the network roadmaps that are able to address resilience requirements are able to withstand challenges longer. Also, challenge response procedures are deployed faster in such networks. In plan resilience management, the focus is to decide the network resilience strategy and put in place a plan for implementing resilience management as part of the roadmap. This process is illustrated in Figure 6-9.

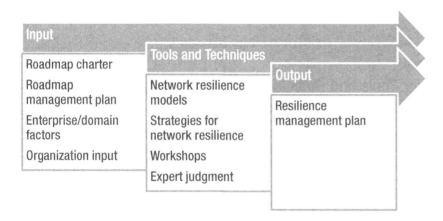

Figure 6-9. Resilience plan management

Plan Resilience Management: Input

Roadmap Charter

As discussed earlier, a roadmap charter provides the bounds and limits for the network roadmap. These inputs help determine the scope of resilience management that can be performed.

Roadmap Management Plan

Once defined, the roadmap management plan gives critical input regarding the following:

- Extent to which resilience has to be managed in the network under development
- Input regarding how resilience management has to be planned

Enterprise or Domain Factors

Enterprise factors could give input regarding:

- The level of resilience management accepted as the norm in the industry
- Resilience management that is being followed by some of the chief competitors
- Input that could be obtained from standards in the domain regarding resilience management

Organization Input

Organizational input could include the following:

- Standards and processes that should be complied with by the resilience management plan
- Input from other products or roadmaps regarding resilience management

Plan Resilience Management: Tools and Techniques

Network Resilience Models

As discussed earlier in this chapter, the resilience models analysis could be used to understand the methods to be adopted for resilience management in the network. These provide the basis for network resilience management and help define the aspects of resilience, with respect to implementing the same in the network roadmap, before deciding on the strategy for handling the same.

■ **Note** Please refer to Chapter 5 for a more detailed analysis of prevalent network resilience models.

Strategies for Network Resilience

The strategy that is adopted for network resilience actually determines:

- The effort spent on resilience management

- The levels of tolerances provided by the network toward various resiliency aspects

- The effectiveness of the network in being able to evolve in case of challenges and other threats.

The strategies for network resilience could be any of those defined among ANSA projects, ATIS, CMU-CERT, SUMOWIN, ResiliNets–D2R2, or resilience control loop.

Note Please refer to Chapter 5 for more details on the network resilience strategies.

Workshops

As discussed earlier, workshops are useful for developing resilience management to bring necessary stakeholders and subject matter experts to brainstorm different options and strategies, to analyze implications, and to implement a plan that would cover all of these aspects and deliver the resilience management plan that is best suited for the network and the organization.

Expert Judgment

As discussed earlier, expert judgment is always necessary to help tune a process and to optimize input obtained when using other techniques. Expert judgment that comes based on years of experience in the domain and in network development is indispensible and, when used well, can make the resilience management plan stronger and appropriate.

Plan Resilience Management: Output

Resilience Management Plan

The principal output of the plan resilience management process is the resilience management plan, which could contain the following critical input regarding how resilience is to be developed and reviewed:

- The aspects of resilience that will be actively developed and managed in the network

- The kinds of challenges to be handled by the network and their priorities

- The resilience management strategy that is chosen and any customizations added to the strategy to adopt to the network under development

- The methods by which resilience will be measured and documented and when theses will be updated

- The ways in which effectiveness of resilience control will be measured and incidents documented for effectiveness

- Triggers based on which resilience strategy will be executed and how these will be monitored

> **Note**   The following processes for resilience definition will depend on the actual resilience strategy that is used. We have given a set of processes based on the common understanding of framework that needs to be developed for network resilience to be defined. It is possible that this may not apply to a specific resilience strategy used by the actual network.

Define Service Levels

To be able to define the resilience strategy, you could start by defining the service levels that are acceptable for the network. Figure 6-10 illustrates this process.

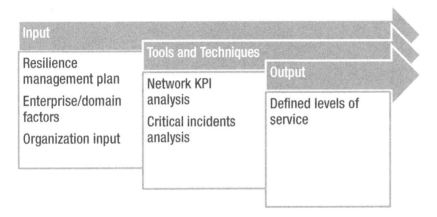

Figure 6-10.   *Definning the service levels*

Define Service Levels: Tools and Techniques

Network KPI Analysis

To define acceptable levels of service, one could start with critical KPIs that determine how the network performance is perceived. Network KPI analysis tries to determine discrete points determined as a combination of KPI levels that give an indication of availability, dependability, reliability, trustworthiness, and other critical aspects of the network.

Critical Incidents Analysis

Analysis of critical incidents when the network was subjected to external challenges could also be a valuable tool to determine how the network behaved and to project service levels based on such behavior.

Define Service Levels: Output

Defined Levels of Service

The output of the define service levels process is the actual levels of service definition, which would include:

- Clearly defined levels of service

- Each level of service characterized and defined by measurable KPIs of the network

- Optionally each level of service could also include vulnerabilities for that level of service and the source for it

Perform Challenge KPI Impact Analysis

To be able to define the resilience strategy, you could start with defining the service levels that are acceptable for the network. Figure 6-11 illustrates this process.

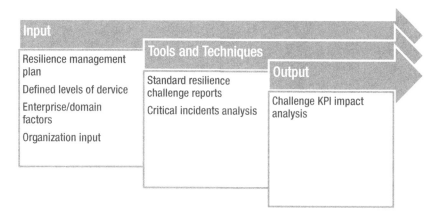

Input

Resilience management plan

Defined levels of dervice

Enterprise/domain factors

Organization input

Tools and Techniques

Standard resilience challenge reports

Critical incidents analysis

Output

Challenge KPI impact analysis

Figure 6-11. *KPI impact analysis*

Perform Challenge KPI Impact Analysis: Tools and Techniques

Standard Resilience Challenge Reports

In most network domains, there are published reports of valid challenges and acceptable strategies of responses for these. Analysis of such reports gives good ideas about which critical KPIs are impacted by the challenges and could contain hints about valid response strategies for these.

Critical Incidents Analysis

As explained earlier, analysis of critical incidents when the network was subjected to external challenges could also be a valuable tool to determine how the network behaved and to understand the KPIs that were impacted during the events.

Perform Challenge KPI Impact Analysis: Output

Challenge KPI Impact Analysis

The output of challenge KPI impact analysis could be:

- A table that presents the service levels, challenges that impact the service level, and the KPIs that are impacted under such challenges
- Optionally, it could also include possible mitigation and prevention strategies

Define Resilience Strategy

Having defined the levels of service and the impact on KPIs by critical challenges, you are ready to define an actual resilience strategy for the network. This process is illustrated in Figure 6-12.

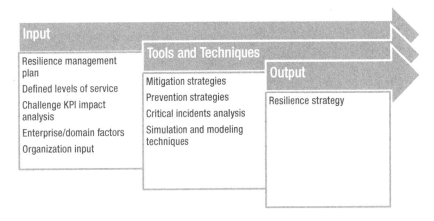

Figure 6-12. *Resilience strategy*

Define Resilience Strategy: Tools and Techniques

Mitigation Strategies

Mitigation strategies include steps that can be taken to recover from the situation or to improve or target a specific level of service including:

- Acceptable strategies such as redeployment of resources

- Proactive reduction of service in some parts of the network

- Proactive communication on the diminished levels of service to all consumers and stakeholders

These are clearly short-term strategies to ensure the impact of challenges is mitigated and acceptable levels of service are recovered as soon as possible.

Prevention Strategies

Prevention strategies are more long term and also take more effort to plan and implement. These could include:

- Structurally improving parts of the system to ensure KPIs are not vulnerable to challenges

- Proactively improving parts of the system that may prove weak to challenges by improving design, algorithm, technologies, or other implementation aspects or using improved antichallenge measures in the system

Simulation and Modeling techniques

The use of simulation techniques is one way to develop models to simulate the network at different levels of service, generate the challenges, and observe the impact on the KPIs. The results could be fed into the model to generate possible measures to mitigate and preempt the challenge. Simulation and modeling require a lot of tooling and domain expertise as well as much effort and cost to set up.

Define Resilience Strategy: Output

Resilience Strategy

The actual resilience strategy as an output should include:

- A table that presents the service levels, challenges that impact the service level, and the KPIs that are impacted under these challenges with mitigation and prevention strategies

- A way to document or review the resilience response and ensure the strategy remains relevant and current

This information becomes input to the roadmap planning and review to ensure resilience is ensured in the roadmap for the levels of service that are targeted.

Perform Network Resilience Review

To be able to define the resilience review strategy, we could start with defining the service levels that are acceptable for the network. Figure 6-13 outlines this process.

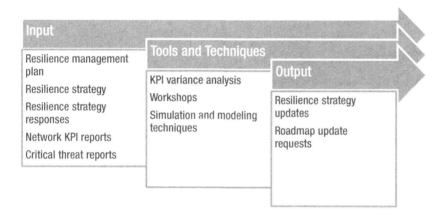

Figure 6-13. *Resilience review strategy*

Perform Network Resilience Review: Input

Resilience Strategy Responses

Input as to how the resilience strategy responses actually worked on the network that is deployed is essential for reviewing the resilience strategy itself.

Network KPI Reports

There should be periodic KPI reports from the network that are deployed with average KPIs, KPI trends, and key KPI variances observed under certain conditions or certain time periods.

Critical Threat Reports

Although average KPIs and KPI trends are more periodic in nature, critical threat reports could be received anytime during the network operations. These need to be taken as input and then trigger a nonperiod resilience review to assess the impact of the threat in real time and evolve the resilience strategy. This should include:

- The nature of the threat or challenge

- The agency or organization that is issuing the report

- The details on the KPIs impacted and assessment of impact on the network

Perform Network Resilience Review: Tools and Techniques

KPI Variance Analysis

The simplest analysis tool would be to compare expected KPI variance based on the challenge and review this with actual KPI variances observed, so that:

- The root cause for the variance could be found

- Remedial actions based on the variance could be reflected in the resilience strategy and also form the basis for roadmap update requests

Simulation and Modeling Techniques

As explained earlier, simulation techniques could be used to compare expected behavior with actual behavior and impact of responses and further fine tune the responses and the resilience strategy.

Perform Network Resilience Review: Output

Resilience Strategy Updates

Based on the review, the actual resilience strategy could be updated to include improved resilience mechanisms or to updated the challenge or threat list based on additional input. Any change to the resilience strategy could initiate roadmap update requests that need to be handled as part of roadmap change control.

Resilience Management Plan Updates

The nature of input received could also initiate updates by the way resilience management is planned.

Plan Operability Management

One of the important aspects of pro-active evolution, as discussed in Chapter 5, is the ability to predict and stay ahead of latest developments and industry trends, which should be incorporated in the network to continue to evolve. We capture input in this category under operability management as well as under the different subcategories of fault, configuration, accounting, performance, and security (FCAPS). This is illustrated in Figure 6-14.

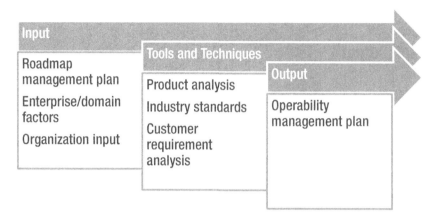

Figure 6-14. *Operability management*

Plan Operability Management: Tools and Techniques

Product Analysis

Under product analysis, as a technique, it is important to understand which critical aspects of the product should be considered under FCAPS to be able to deliver and evolve a roadmap of good quality, including items like:

- Support for the latest logging techniques
- Requirements for troubleshooting issues remotely
- Ability to monitor critical statistics of system functionality
- Ability to collect real-time performance data

Industry Standards

Industry standards could include well-accepted baselines that networks should be compliant with. These include:

- Competitor network analysis
- Deployment and operational baselines that could be prevailing in the industry

Customer Requirement Analysis

Customers could also have specific requirements that need to be satisfied as part of the operability requirements, including

- Specific features that are required for regulatory or compliance aspects

- Features that are required to cover deployment and acceptance tests from network vendors

- Operational implications derived by customers from their past network analysis

Plan Operability Management: Output

Operability Management Plan

We define the operability management plan as the single source for all information related to aspects of operability that act as input for roadmap evolution, including:

- Operability aspects that are to be targeted by the network, including ways to baseline different aspects of operability

- Information about stakeholders that are responsible for operability aspects of the network

- Information about how aspects of operability are to be monitored for evolving processes and how these should be tracked from industry sources, trade publications, standard bodies, and other networking groups of importance

- Process steps about how requirements to operability improvement are to be collected and reviewed as part of the roadmap review process

Summary

It has been our endeavor throughout this chapter to illustrate how a set of processes could be defined under a framework to ensure that the network roadmap stays updated, relevant, and continues to evolve as per changes in the business, market, and industry conditions. As mentioned in Chapter 5, processes and tools are only useful to the extent that they guide the user to think in certain ways. It is the user who needs to be motivated enough to think on the same lines. The most important reason for you to do so may be that, like all human tendencies, the tendency to improve oneself is the most far-reaching in terms of advancement of human prowess. We expect that the process of evolution of network roadmaps will help make the network better in itself, and at the time and to help it evolve and keep itself relevant, effective, and able to meet business needs.

Index

M

N

O

Get the eBook for only $10!

Now you can take the weightless companion with you anywhere, anytime. Your purchase of this book entitles you to 3 electronic versions for only $10.

This Apress title will prove so indispensible that you'll want to carry it with you everywhere, which is why we are offering the eBook in 3 formats for only $10 if you have already purchased the print book.

Convenient and fully searchable, the PDF version enables you to easily find and copy code—or perform examples by quickly toggling between instructions and applications. The MOBI format is ideal for your Kindle, while the ePUB can be utilized on a variety of mobile devices.

Go to www.apress.com/promo/tendollars to purchase your companion eBook.

Apress®
THE EXPERT'S VOICE™